# SKILFUL HANDS

# SKILFUL HANDS

Studies in the Life of David

# RAYMOND BROWN

M.A., M.Th., Ph.D.

*He chose David also his servant*
*and took him from the sheepfolds.*
*So he . . . guided them by the*
*skilfulness of his hands.*

Psalm 78: 70, 72

**LAKELAND**
BLUNDELL HOUSE
GOODWOOD ROAD
LONDON SE14 6BL

ISBN 0 551 00248 4

Made and printed in Great Britain by
Cox & Wyman Ltd,
London, Reading and Fakenham

# CONTENTS

To my friends at
**UPTON VALE BAPTIST CHURCH, TORQUAY**
with affectionate gratitude

# INTRODUCTION

David was the most outstanding king of Old Testament times. In the biblical narratives some Hebrew monarchs are briefly dismissed in two or three verses, but the story of David spans forty chapters. Old Testament writers of later periods made special mention of him, and many of their treasured hopes regarding an ultimate national deliverer and spiritual hero became associated with his name. But David's life-story is far from being mere history; it offers a series of important practical lessons for the believer today. Firstly, they have an obvious *intellectual importance*. Every biblical story has been recorded "for our instruction" (Rom. 15:4 NEB). In another place (1 Cor. 10:11) the apostle Paul says that all the events of Old Testament times "happened unto them for ensamples: and they are written for our admonition". Our minds need to be carefully stored with the truths of God. All too often we make mistakes in the Christian life simply because we do not *know* what God expects of us. We do well to remember that the word "disciple" simply means "learner", and so David's life ought to say something to us intellectually. Clearly there are truths here that we need to grasp if we are to go on with God.

Further, these Old Testament narratives have rich *emotional value*. Man needs something more than a lesson. He wants a Companion. In many of life's experiences the exact truth to be grasped is all too obvious but the heart cries out for comfort, understanding and help. Sometimes we cannot think how we are going to get through some particular spell of unhappiness, grief or distress, but these magnificent stories of the Bible offer endless encouragement as they show us just how well many of these great characters coped with their difficulties and troubles. J. B. Phillips offers this helpful paraphrase of Paul's words in Romans 15:4 ". . . that when we read in the scriptures of the endurance of men and of all the help God gave them in those days, we may be encouraged to go on hoping in our time." These stories may well enable us to face life again, knowing that the God who helped others in the past is the God who helps us now.

Finally, these stories provide us with what we might describe as *volitional incentive*. They help to shake us out of our careless inertia and drive us to action. It is not enough simply to receive a truth into our minds, and welcome God's comfort to our hearts. There are certain things that we must *do* for God. He is referred to in the following verse (Rom. 15:5) as "the source of all fortitude" (NEB) and He is pleased to use these stories to strengthen our wills for resolute action.

The biblical passages take us to an exceptionally restless period of Hebrew history during which Israel badly needed a leader of rich and exemplary devotion. Things had become hopelessly chaotic under Saul, the first man to occupy the throne of Israel, and it is obviously necessary for us to look in the first place at this disappointing king.

# I

# A DISAPPOINTING KING

Saul is a stark illustration of the man of high promise who fails to realize God's lofty purpose for his life. The account of his reign is probably one of the most dismal stories in the whole of Scripture. Nobody could have guessed that he would be such a dreadful failure. His story is related in Scripture as a warning. It illustrates the principle that whenever a man sins it is not a solitary or isolated event. Inevitably, all our transgressions have a triple effect. First of all, we sin against God. David gave eloquent expression to this: "Against thee, thee only, have I sinned, and done this evil in thy sight: that thou mightest be justified when thou speakest, and be clear when thou judgest" (Ps. 51:4). We also sin against others. Even if it is something about which nobody else knows anything, it will ultimately affect other people. Even our so-called secret sins will slowly and subtly lower our standards so that we shall not be the effective witnesses that we ought to be. Finally, we sin against our better selves. It is obvious, of course, that sin has seriously defaced the divine image in man, but we are not left without high standards, noble resolves and spiritual ambitions. Every time we transgress, we sin against these lofty principles and rich ideals. We consider Saul's story under these three aspects of failure: his sin against God, against his fellows, and against himself. His tragic life was:

I A DISAPPOINTMENT TO GOD
God called this exceptionally gifted man to an office of immense spiritual responsibility. He was to be Israel's first king. In many ways, Saul was born for such a task, but he

made the all too common mistake of living entirely to himself. Time and again, in the early narratives, we meet that cruel appeal to self-satisfaction and it is as though he could not escape the awful compulsion to obey it. Knowing the failure of his reign, there is something dreadfully pathetic about those words in 1 Samuel 9:15ff.: "Now the Lord had told Samuel in his ear a day before Saul came, saying, Tomorrow about this time I will send thee a man out of the land of Benjamin, and thou shalt anoint him to be captain over my people Israel, that he may save my people out of the hand of the Philistines: for I have looked upon my people, because their cry is come unto me. And when Samuel saw Saul, the Lord said unto him, Behold the man whom I spake to thee of! this same shall reign over my people." Think again of the divine intention for Saul's life: "captain . . . that he may save"; captain over the people of God, their saviour in a time of trouble. But the captain became a captive to his own selfish desires and changing moods, and the intended saviour became a tragic failure.

(a) *Saul became a tragic disappointment to the God who chose him*
God's good hand had been upon him throughout his earlier life and it was the Lord's purpose to use him in a most responsible position of leadership (1 Sam. 9:15-17; 10:1). The tragedy of Saul is that, though he knew that God had great plans for him, he allowed his own selfishness to rob him of the greater joy of pleasing God. John Hunt, a missionary in the last century to the cannibals of Fiji, once put it this way: writing to a missionary colleague about "holiness" he urged his friend to join him in the prayer that they would "escape the curse of a useless life". God had rich purposes for Saul's life but it ended in tragedy. The life of useful possibilities was spoiled by the pursuit of useless things.

## (b) Saul was a disappointment to the God who equipped him

No man is sent into service without the requisite abilities and qualities. Sometimes these only come in the exercise of the ministry itself. They are not necessarily given in advance, nor are we provided with reserve supplies. The biblical story makes it obvious that Saul was physically equipped for the task (1 Sam. 9:2). He is described as "a choice young man, and a goodly" and appears to have been one of the most handsome (RSV) as well as the tallest among the men of Israel. Without doubt he was intellectually equipped. He had plenty of sound common sense and, as we shall see later, he knew how to handle delicate and difficult situations. He was also spiritually equipped. He gave himself to the discipline of hearing God's Word (1 Sam. 9:27) and seems to have been deeply concerned about spiritual things. Yet, although he began in this way, his promising life took the wrong turning and he became a bitter disappointment to the God who had thrust him into a magnificent opportunity for service.

## (c) Saul also disappointed the God who loved him

This is the dreadful thing about sin: God must be so grieved by it. He loves us so much and longs that our lives might be profitable and enriching to others. He is disappointed when we fall short of the high standards and great plans that He has for our lives. But, despite Saul's failure and rejection as king, God went on caring for him, protecting him in times of danger and striving to bring him to repentance and trust. It is true, of course, that he lost his power as a leader (1 Sam. 16:14) but God continued to plead with him just as He pleads with us when we fail. If Saul had kept his priorities right it might well have been so different. His could have been a truly magnificent reign but it went down in the annals of Hebrew history as a period of shattered hopes and frustrated intentions.

Saul was not fit to lead. His sins were to have a corrupting influence upon his fellow-countrymen. There were seven tragic sins in Saul's life in this early period. We shall look at 1 Samuel, chapters 13-15, and see where this man made his mistakes. It seems as though all was going well until the incident recorded in 1 Samuel 13:8ff. We shall consider the narrative from this point onwards.

(a) Saul's spiritual decline probably began with *impatience*. He could not wait for God, and power seems to have gone to his head. He had become accustomed to people running in all directions to please him and was not used to waiting for anybody or anything. At this particular time (1 Sam. 13:8-14) Samuel was expected to visit Gilgal in order to offer the sacrifice. After a full week of waiting the prophet still had not appeared, and so Saul took matters into his own hands: "*He* offered the burnt offering." The people knew that this was Samuel's task and, moreover, Saul knew that he had made a mistake. Just as he had finished officiating, Samuel appeared on the scene, and Saul began to make excuses: "I saw the people were scattered from me . . . I forced myself therefore and offered a burnt offering" (1 Sam. 13:11f).

If we genuinely long to walk in unbroken fellowship with God, we must guard against this sin of impatience. There are various places in Scripture where we are urged to wait upon God (Ps. 37:7; 62:1; Lam. 3:25f; Hab. 2:1-3) and the truly committed Christian refuses to be hurried into actions that might well dishonour God, and possibly bring distress to others. Remember that the *Acts of the Apostles* starts not with activity but with passivity. It begins with a story about people who obeyed the Lord by waiting (Luke 24:49; Acts 1:4). This was something Saul could not do. The apostle Paul believed that power was given to believing people in order to make them patient (Col. 1:11). Not many months after I became a Christian, I asked a Christian friend to write something in the front of my first study Bible. Her message to me that day has stayed with me ever since. She wrote out

Hebrews 10:36 in Moffat's translation: "Steady patience is what you need" and she underlined the "you"! She knew me better than I knew myself! That blunt statement has stayed with me over the years, and it contains a clear message to us all. Saul knew very well that it was not his responsibility to offer the burnt offering. His duties did not lie in that realm at all but he refused to wait until Samuel arrived.

(b) The sin of impatience soon led on to that of *presumption*. The person who insists on plotting his own course in life is not deeply sensitive to what is right or wrong before God. 1 Samuel 13:13-14 continues the story: "Thou hast done foolishly," says Samuel to Saul, "thou has not kept the commandment of the Lord thy God which He commanded thee." His impatience had led him to presumption. The Word of God urges us to come before the Lord with boldness and confidence, but we must take care that our boldness does not degenerate into irreverence and presumption. Saul lacked all sense of awe and worship. There is another equally pathetic story of an Old Testament king who presumed to take upon himself the duties of a divinely appointed officiant at worship. Uzziah, the king who was "marvellously helped, till he was strong" also came to a tragic end (2 Chr. 26:15-21).

(c) The next sin is that of *greed*. Israel's first king turned into an avaricious materialist. Look at the story in 1 Samuel 15. The prophet Samuel approached Saul with a divine command. It seems as though he is almost given another chance "Now therefore hearken thou unto the voice of the words of the Lord" (15:1). In a military encounter with the Amalekites he is clearly told that the spoil must be devoted to God, but he does not do what he is commanded. "But Saul and the people spared Agag, and the best of the sheep, and of the oxen, and of the fatlings, and the lambs, and all that was good, and would not utterly destroy them: but every thing that was vile and refuse; that they destroyed utterly" (1 Sam. 15:9). They only "devoted" (RV) to the Lord that which they did not want for themselves. Such are the ways of a greedy man. There was a later Old Testament prophet who had something to say about this kind of thing. It was Malachi, you will remember, who pressed this point home, many centuries after Saul: "And if ye offer the blind for sacrifice, is it not evil? and if ye offer the lame and sick, is it not evil? offer it now unto thy governor; will he be pleased with thee or accept thy person?" (Mal. 1:8). The prophet is asking whether their earthly leaders would be pleased with that which they are content to give to their Heavenly Father. He goes on to assert that in this way the people are robbing God (Mal. 3:8). Materialism is one of the sins of our age and Christians are not free from its perils. Those who love God with all their hearts must guard their minds and spirits against this sin of putting their own interests and comfort first and thinking more of their own possessions than they do of Him. This is what the thoroughly worldly man does; he attends first to his own needs. Saul allowed a few choice-looking sheep to rob him of immense spiritual blessing and lasting joy and we must take care lest the lust for material things robs us of deep and abiding spiritual satisfaction.

(d) Of course, all this arose because of *disobedience*. This was obviously the most serious of Saul's failures. We have noticed it already in 1 Samuel 13:13-14: "Thou hast not kept the commandment of the Lord." It occurs again in the sad story in 1 Samuel 15. The word that came to Samuel was that the Lord repented that Saul was king: "for he is turned back from following me, and hath not performed my commandments." The man who does not maintain his communion with God is not likely to offer his obedience to God. It is all the more sad in view of the fact that right at the beginning of that fateful day he had been warned about the dangers of disobedience (15:1). He heard the serious warning but as the day wore on what he *saw* meant more to him than what he had *heard* from God. Samuel is grieved about Saul's sin of tragic disobedience and says: "to obey is better than sacrifice and *to hearken* than the fat of rams."

(e) There is also the sin of *hypocrisy*. During the day Saul

14

had become a thief; he had stolen that which really belonged to God. Then he showed himself to be a liar as well. Listen to his first words as he meets the heartbroken prophet: "Blessed be thou of the Lord: I have performed the commandment of the Lord." What a terrible lie. Saul had all the right jargon. He was not short of a choice phrase or two. Even when challenged by Samuel with the fact of his sin he protested yet again: "Yea, I have obeyed the voice of the Lord" (15:20). The word "hypocrite" comes from a term the Greeks used in theatrical circles, and it described someone wearing a mask. This is exactly what Saul was doing that day. He was trying to convince Samuel that he was a godly man, but Samuel had already been warned by God that Saul was merely displaying a mask. We need something more than words if we are to convince others of our genuine loyalty to God.

(f) *Pride* was the next of Saul's sins which Samuel had to expose. The distressed prophet could see it all quite clearly. He looked into Saul's eyes and said, "When thou wast little in thine own sight, wast thou not made the head of the tribes of Israel?" (1 Sam. 15:17). God keep us small in our own sight. There are probably more disasters over this than almost anything else. Think of the continually repeated warnings of the apostle Paul about this devastating evil (Rom. 12:10, 16; Phil. 2:3). It is so easy to become "puffed up". This is exactly what happened to Saul. Power corrupted.

(g) *Cowardice* comes next. This is one of the things one dislikes most about him. He made sure that he put the blame for all this sin on to other people. Saul had repeatedly ignored the divine commandment. The least he could do was to acknowledge that it was his failure and face the consequences. Instead, he tried to put the responsibility on to others. When Samuel heard the bleating of the sheep at that dramatic moment of meeting, Saul was quick to say "*They* have brought them from the Amalekites: for *the people* spared the best of the sheep and the oxen" (1 Sam. 15:15). He repeats it again as the conversation continues: "But *the people* took of the spoil" (15:21), and then he ultimately makes the pathetic confession: "I have transgressed the commandment of the Lord, and thy words *because I feared the people*, and obeyed their voice" (15:24). What words from a king! He stood head and shoulders above everyone else so that every man and woman in Israel literally had to look up to him, and yet he said "I was afraid of what these people might say or do to me, therefore I acted in this way." What cowardice.

### 3 A GRIEF TO HIMSELF

Saul failed God and the people. He also let himself down. Israel's tallest king finished up its greatest fool. In a later chapter he calls out in unrelieved anguish: "I have played the fool and have erred exceedingly" (1 Sam. 26:21). Life is such a rich opportunity for us to glorify God. Think of the words of our majestic Lord: "I have glorified thee on the earth: I have finished the work which thou gavest me to do" (John 17:4). Saul could not end his days like that: "I have glorified thee on the earth." He could only have said "I have dishonoured thee on the earth." How will it be with us? When the apostle Paul wrote to the Corinthians about these important stories of Old Testament times, he said that they were recorded "for our admonition" and he went on to sound this note of serious appeal: "Wherefore let him that thinketh he standeth take heed lest he fall" (1. Cor. 10:11f).

It we are to present a balanced account of Saul's life, it is necessary for us to look with equal seriousness at some of the lovely qualities with which Saul began his work for God, even though he later threw them over.

(a) At the beginning he was a man *endued with great humility*. At their first meeting Samuel told Saul of the work that God had for him to do but young Saul answered, "Am not I a Benjamite, of the smallest of the tribes of Israel and my family the least of all the families of the tribe of Benjamin? Wherefore then speakest thou so to me?" (1 Sam. 9:21). Notice his protestation of absolute unworthiness: I am a *poor* member of the *least* of the families of the *smallest* tribe. Later on came the moment for the public declaration of his kingship but when they looked for the man chosen to be the first king of Israel he could not be found anywhere. After earnest prayer about his whereabouts, the word came from the Lord: "Behold, he hath hid himself among the stuff" (10:22). Here was no self-exaltation, rather a deep sense of personal unworthiness and a desire to shrink from the solemn and demanding responsibilities of kingship. Yet think how he changed.

(b) Further, in those early days, *he knew what it was to attend to the word of God*. Notice the details recorded in 1 Samuel 9:25ff.: "Samuel communed with Saul upon the top of the house." The following morning before be became preoccupied with all the problems of leadership, economic difficulties, political tensions, military manoeuvres, the prophet said a word to him that comes to us also across the centuries: "Stand thou still a while, that I may show thee the word of God" (9:27). Do we ever take time to "stand still" amidst a busy life just so that we can receive the guidance and commandment of the Lord God, or do we plunge ourselves into fresh responsibilities and demanding assignments without even seeking His mind about them?

(c) Remember too that *Saul's faith was once confirmed by miraculous signs*. Read I Samuel 10:1-6 again. After Saul had been anointed by the prophet and had acknowledged the sovereign control of God over his life, he began to witness a series of astonishing events. He was told that he would meet two men at a specified place; he was clearly informed as to what they would say upon meeting him. He was then informed by Samuel of the next encounter that would be his, whom he would meet and what the men would be doing. Later still he was told that he would meet a group of wandering prophets and that the Spirit of the Lord would come down upon him in mighty power. These three events were to be used to confirm his divine appointment and so rob him of any sense of spiritual uncertainty or natural fear.

(d) Notice this also, *he was a man who experienced the presence of God in his life*. The miraculous signs could be regarded as confirmation of the divine presence. What glorious words with which to begin any project or service for the Lord: "God is with thee" (1 Sam. 10:7). He went on his way with that stirring word of assurance ringing in his ears. Yet in a later chapter, following his fatal sins of greed, disobedience and rebellion, it is said of Saul that the Spirit of the Lord departed from him (1 Sam. 16:14; cf. 18:12).

(e) Moreover, at the beginning of his career *Saul exercised great self-control*. This, one of Saul's most endearing qualities, is illustrated in the incident recorded in 1 Samuel 10:26f. Once acknowledged as king, Saul returned to his native town followed by a group of his closest subjects, but some of the inhabitants refused to recognize his kingship. They sneered and said "How shall this man save us? And they despised him and brought him no presents. *But he held his peace*" or, as the margin puts it, "was as though he had been deaf". What a splendid thing to do that day, and what a tragedy that he could not keep it up. What a pity he did not act in the same way on the day when those thoughtless women came out singing in celebration of David's victory over Goliath. In that moment Saul ought to have recalled his entry into Gibeah and made "as though he had been deaf". So much tragedy stemmed from that song.

(f) At the start of his reign *Saul was eager to confess his absolute reliance upon God*. Look at 1 Samuel 11:12f.: some blood-thirsty soldiers wanted Samuel to order the execution of all those who had refused to fight alongside them. "Bring the men," they said, "that we may put them to death." But Saul intervened and would not allow them to act in this way: "There shall not a man be put to death this day: for today *the Lord* hath wrought salvation in Israel." Saul says in effect: "This is God's work. Any victory we have obtained is due to His goodness alone. I have depended entirely upon Him and He has not disappointed me. This is no moment for vindictive behaviour."

It is important to stress the fact that Saul started his work for God in a most exemplary manner. At the beginning he relied upon the Lord, but he did not continue as he began. We should recall the serious words in Romans 11:20 (NEB): "Put away your pride and be on your guard."

# 2

# GOD'S MAN FOR DIFFICULT TIMES

Samuel is one of those magnificent characters in Scripture who are content to fill a minor role. He was a man willing to be used by God for the greater blessing of someone else. Without his influence, it is unlikely that David would have made such a deep impresssion upon the spiritual life of the nation. We note three important things about Samuel:

*(a) His work was not easy*
As a child, Samuel had been given a difficult task (1 Sam. 3:11-18). That kind of arduous and embarrassing mission had to be repeated more than once throughout his prophetic ministry. He knew from the sad example of Eli that uncorrected transgression is an added grief to God and so when he was sent to King Saul with a word of rebuke, "he told him every whit and hid nothing from him." Read 1 Samuel chapters 12 to 15, and note how many times Samuel had to reprove the king as well as the people. His faithfulness to God's word might easily have cost him his life, but he listened for the divine voice and went obediently to the royal house with words of warning and judgment. It cannot have been easy. Perhaps God is calling you to some task, and you shrink from it because you know it will be extremely difficult. Think of the heroes of the past. Scripture is packed with magnificent stories of men and women who were not naturally courageous but who proved that God gives the strength we need as we obey His summons. Some hard work is part of every believer's sanctification. Richard Baxter put

it like this: "Reader, heaven is above thee, and dost thou think to travel this steep ascent without labour and resolution? Canst thou get that earthly heart to heaven, and bring that backward mind to God, while thou liest still and takest thine ease? If lying down at the foot of a hill, and looking toward the top and wishing we were there, would serve the turn, then we should have daily travellers for heaven. As the sluggard that stretches himself on his bed and cries, O that this were working! so doest thou talk, and trifle and live at thine ease and say, O that I could get my heart to heaven! How many read books and hear sermons, expecting to hear of some easier way, or to meet with a shorter course to comfort than they are ever likely to find in Scripture? Or they ask for directions for a heavenly life, and if the hearing them will serve, they will be heavenly Christians; but if we show them their work, and tell them they cannot have these delights on easier terms, then they leave us, as the young man left Christ, sorrowful." (*The Saint's Everlasting Rest*)

### (b) His work was not selfish

Samuel had very little to gain personally from his service for God. He was an old man by the time Saul's disobedience was becoming obvious (1 Sam. 12:2), and might well have preferred to keep silent about the distressing sins and obvious failures of the royal house. He was not going to benefit very much even if a new king came to the throne; his days were numbered. But Samuel knew that God had given him a task to perform and he did it faithfully even though he realized he would get very little out of it personally. He would at least be able to treasure the satisfaction that he had obeyed God and done those things that would please the Lord.

### (c) His work was not spectacular

Samuel rarely comes to the centre of the stage in this period of history. He had an essential but minor part in the unfolding purposes of God for His people. This kind of attitude is typical of the saints. They are happy to fulfil any role for God. They are not in the least bit interested in human recognition or earthly approbation. Their ambition is a far nobler one. They aim to please God and are particularly delighted if God uses them to bring greater blessing to someone else. But because Samuel's work was not spectacular, we do not mean to say that it was not important. For one thing Samuel exercised an unapplauded ministry in the secret place of prayer. Look at the words of the prophet in 1 Samuel 12:23: "Moreover as for me, God forbid that I should sin against the Lord in ceasing to pray for you . . ." P. T. Forsyth used to say that all sin can be traced to prayerlessness. Samuel would have agreed with that, but his prayer-ministry was not a limelight task. He just got on with it, trusting that God would use his sceret intercessions for the ultimate blessing of those needy people.

But Samuel was not without his difficulties, and we turn now to a study of 1 Samuel 16:1-13, the familiar account of the anointing of David at Bethlehem. The narrative offers some illuminating insights into the problems which Samuel had to face and overcome, and we note some of the areas of personal experience in which Samuel had to battle.

1 DEPRESSION

Naturally, Samuel had hoped that things would work out well under Saul's leadership and he was bitterly disappointed when Israel's first king turned out to be such a tragic failure. Prophet and king parted company, but Samuel grieved over Saul's disobedience (1 Sam. 15:35). But God knew that the situation had to be rectified and spoke clearly to Samuel: "How long wilt thou mourn for Saul, seeing I have rejected him from reigning over Israel?" (1 Sam. 16:1). Although the Lord could understand Samuel's grief, it was not His purpose for the old prophet to continue in his agonizing mental and spiritual distress. God had already made other plans for the leadership of the nation. As Samuel wept in Ramah, the Lord God was moving in the heart of a young shepherd on the hills of Bethlehem. We must never allow our external circumstances to cast us into utter despair. We only know *part* of the story. Remember that whilst we are worrying about our present problems God is already planning something for us about which at present we know nothing. Samuel would hardly have continued sighing at Ramah if he could have heard the exultant voice of that young lad singing on the hills of Bethlehem. Our limited vision often causes us to think that we have been forgotten, but He knows the precise moment at which to introduce that important factor which will change our outlook and transform our situation.

## 2 FEAR

Samuel also had to battle against fear. He was clearly told that the Lord had chosen a king from among the sons of Jesse (1 Sam. 16:3) but Samuel was terrified at the thought of anointing a successor to Saul in a semi-public way. "How can I go?" he says. "If Saul hear it, he will kill me" (1 Sam. 16:2). It now becomes obvious that Samuel is not only grieved about Saul; he is frightened of him as well, yet in the previous chapter he hardly gives the impression of being a fearful man. His words of rebuke and condemnation ring out clearly and confidently: "What meaneth then this bleating of the sheep in mine ears ... to obey is better than sacrifice ... For rebellion is as the sin of witchcraft, and stubbornness is as iniquity and idolatry" (1 Sam. 15:14, 22f.). It seems as though this normally courageous man became suddenly afraid when he thought of the possible reaction of Saul when he heard the news of the anointing. This is one of the terribly sad things about depression: some of our best qualities leave us. The man who is normally fearless becomes terribly frightened. We see this in the life of Elijah. The man who boldly confronted the Baal-prophets on Mount Carmel was later terrified at the thought of being arrested and slain by a godless queen (1 Kings 18:19ff.; 19:1ff.).

But notice how gently and graciously the Lord deals with

Samuel's fear. He comes to meet him *where he is and as he is*. Quietly and with such reassurance the Lord says: "Take an heifer with thee, and say, I am come to sacrifice to the Lord. And call Jesse to the sacrifice, and I will shew thee what thou shalt do . . ." (1 Sam. 16:2f.). Samuel is distressed at the thought of walking into Bethlehem with the sole purpose of publicly anointing the next king, so God says, "Just go out on one of your routine sacrificial journeys." Nobody would think this strange and God promises that, as a particular family come before the prophet for the usual ritual presentation prior to the sacrifice, the new divinely-appointed king would be made known to him. God actually accommodated Himself to the anxieties and worries of Samuel. He robbed him of his dread and enabled him to go to Bethlehem with a mind released from worry. How gracious of God to meet Samuel's need in this way. He is just as kind to us and fully understands our frailty (cf. 1 Cor. 10:13 RSV).

### 3 IMPATIENCE

Samuel had a further area of conflict; the Lord had to say some serious things to him about his tendency to impatience. God had told him quite clearly that He would reveal the right man to him (1 Sam. 16:3). All Samuel had to do was wait for the quiet whisper of the divine voice within his own heart and not make hasty judgments himself. But it all seemed so slow that day in Bethlehem. One after another these promising sons of Jesse stood before the anxious prophet until at last he found himself looking up to Eliab who towered above him. Is there a note of impatience as the prophet sighs and says to himself: "Surely the Lord's anointed is before him?" God had said in effect "I will name him" and Samuel only had to *listen*, but like ourselves he thought all the responsibility fell upon his own shoulders. When the voice of God was not heard, he became anxious and fretful; untrusting and unspiritual impatience took over and he found himself thinking that possibly God had overlooked Eliab, the most likely candidate for kingship. He saw the tallest of Jesse's sons, thought how similar he was to Saul in stature and, therefore, eminently suitable for the throne of Israel. But Saul's stature and physical strength had not got the nation very far. How strange that Samuel, of all people, should view this matter from such an unspiritual point of view. Yet we do the same kind of thing. We become frightfully impatient when things do not work out as quickly as we want them to. When God tells us to *wait*, we should do so. Guidance does not always come at exactly the moment we demand it. God often reveals His purposes for our lives a step at a time. He works out all the various stages perfectly. All too often we make the mistake of taking things into our own hands instead of relying on Him for the right moment. God was not in a hurry that day; His man was yet to appear.

## 4 WORLDLINESS

Let us now look at Samuel's fourth mistake. He was misled by the sin of looking at all this from the world's view-point—that is by the standard of appearances. The prophet looked at Eliab, towering above the rest, and thought how fine he would look as king. But Samuel had to learn that God was not looking for a tall man, but a *good* one, and His man was out on the hills of Bethlehem, caring for the sheep. Of course, God gives us our intellects so that we can think things through but every Christian knows that he must sub-ject his own mind to the mind of God. There are serious limitations to our insight and understanding. God does not always choose to act according to the principles of our reason, indeed at times He does things which appear totally unreasonable. The familiar story from the Acts of the Apostles, chapter 8, perfectly illustrates this principle. The Spirit of God was obviously using Philip's preaching, and all the neighbouring towns and villages were feeling the impact of revival. Then, suddenly, Philip was told to leave this spiritually prosperous situation and go out into the desert wastes along by the main trade route from Jerusalem to

Gaza. Humanly speaking, it all seemed so ridiculous, and utterly unreasonable. But God knew that it was more important at that moment for the persuasive evangelist to meet an Ethiopian state official than to preach to the multitudes in the Samaritan villages. What is more, God was counting on Philip's immediate obedience, for at that precise moment a bewildered seeker was making his way home to Ethiopia and God needed an evangelist in the desert. Similarly, Samuel had to learn a great truth as he looked into the face of Eliab. The voice of God sounded clearly through his bewildered mind: "Look not on his countenance, or on the height of his stature; because I have refused him: for the Lord seeth not as man seeth; for man looketh on the outward appearance, but the Lord looketh on the heart" (1 Sam. 16:7). God was looking at Eliab's heart not his height, and He knew how totally unsuitable he was for leadership. It was to the Corinthian church that, in his first letter, Paul claimed that God had always chosen the most unlikely people, the weak and insignificant, for His purposes "that no flesh should glory in His presence" (1 Cor. 1:29). The base things and the despised, the things which are not, are more likely to be used than the arrogant and self-assured. Their story may not reach the headlines or be noted by the multitudes of this world, but they are used by the God who glories in weak things. God's man for that particular situation in Israel was looking after his father's sheep, singing his songs of trust and victory. The moment he was brought before Samuel, the voice of God was clearly heard and Samuel was not in the slightest doubt about it: "Arise, anoint him: for *this is he*." The young shepherd was a man after God's own heart. This is of greater importance than all else.

# 3

# THREE VICTORIES IN ONE DAY

Our previous chapters have considered both Saul and Samuel. We come now to David himself, and begin with what is possibly the greatest scene in his life—the story of his encounter with the Philistine giant, Goliath. Most of us have known and loved the story from childhood but we are probably accustomed to the idea that there was only one conquest that day in the Valley of Elah. In fact, there were three, and it is likely that the great victory over Goliath was only possible because of the two earlier victories. Perhaps we will never be victorious against the Goliaths of our lives until we learn to conquer the not so obvious enemies. Let us turn then to this wonderful narrative in 1 Samuel 17, think again about this magnificent theme of conquest, and seek to apply these things to our own Christian lives. In three different meetings that day young David was confronted with temptation.

1 VICTORY OVER THE TONGUE—*the meeting with Eliab* (1 Sam. 17:22-30)
Jesse was an old man (17:12) and, concerned about the welfare of his three eldest sons who had gone to the battle, he sent young David with necessary provisions for his brothers and with a supply of food for the captain of their regiment (17.18). On arriving at the military encampment David was astonished to notice the fear of the Israelite soldiers. Goliath's threats had obviously terrified them. The whole camp seemed to have lost its nerve. He could not understand it. Although young, his faith was strong and he was deeply convinced that God was wonderfully sufficient.

27

As he heard of the giant's taunts, David became concerned about the reproach of Israel (17:26). After all, they professed to serve "the living God" and, if their God was alive, why were His soldiers in such distress of mind? In David's view the name of God was in danger of being dishonoured among the heathen. How could the Israelites convince their Philistine oppressors of the might of Jehovah if He could not be trusted to deliver them from their enemies (1 Sam. 17:26)?

The battalions who served under Saul were pathetically weak because they lacked a godly leader. As Goliath came striding through the valley he called out "I defy the armies of Israel this day; give me a man, that we may fight together" (17:10), but we read that "when Saul and all Israel heard those words of the Philistine, they were dismayed, and greatly afraid" (17:11; cf. 17:24). Fear follows hard on the heels of unbelief. If we do not trust God, how can we ever hope to be valiant and strong? In his earlier days Saul had led his troops through a score of dangerous military encounters, but now he is powerless and terrified. Only the young messenger from Bethlehem could assess the situation with realism and hope. As David quietly reflected, he knew that immense spiritual issues were at stake here; this was a conflict of faith. Two opposing nations were giving expression to their profound spiritual beliefs and ideals. Dagon was the Philistine deity and it looked as though he was about to triumph. The Philistines would obviously regard Goliath's victory as a clear indication of Jehovah's failure to cope with difficulties.

David knew that the enemy's blasphemous mockery was an offence to God and he became sure that in the strength of Jehovah, he could be a conqueror. At the critical moment when he was about to offer his services, the first temptation of the day came upon him—totally unexpectedly. Eliab, Jesse's eldest son, had been listening to the eager enquiries of his younger brother. The lad's radiant faith suddenly became an offence to him. Tall as he was, Eliab was obviously not big enough for this job. When he saw Goliath's massive frame his faith was as poor as anyone else's. What a mercy Samuel had listened to the warning voice of God at Bethlehem. God knew the cowardly heart that was hidden behind that strong physical frame. No wonder Eliab was angry with David. Spiritual confidence is always an embarrassment to those who are weak in faith and so he turned sharply on his youngest brother and made fun of him: "With whom hast thou left those few sheep in the wilderness?" (1 Sam. 17:28). Like all cowards, he enjoyed having a joke at the expense of someone he regarded as his inferior, whilst all the time he lacked the moral strength to tackle someone like Goliath himself. "I know thy pride," he calls out to David, "and the naughtiness of thine heart" (17:28). The man who lacks faith in God is quick to discern the failings of others. He is always ready with an accusing finger. Whilst he is busy pointing out other people's sins he is not facing up to his own. Eliab's pride was the problem, not David's. Imagine this mere boy being anointed instead of him! So, in his anger Eliab turned on him, but David won his first victory of the day. He knew how to control his temper and master his tongue. He conquered the natural inclination to retaliate. Think what a teenage lad might have said to his great hulking brother overwhelmed with fear! Instead he proved the power of God to see him through an embarrassing moment and turned quietly away to talk with someone else: "he turned from him toward another" (17:29-30). The first battle of the day was over!

The failure to control the tongue is at the root of a good deal of spiritual disaster—for us and for others. If we cannot control our speech, we will not easily control anything else (cf. Jas. 1:26; 3:1-18; Proverbs 10:11, 19; 11:9, 12; 12:13, 18, 23). A famous poster widely displayed during the last war used to say "Careless talk costs lives". The government was concerned about the foolish conversation of people who might easily leak official secrets and bring disaster upon innocent millions. That war is over but the words remain a challenge for those of us who are engaged in Christian warfare. Many a soul has been dreadfully wounded by a hasty word which might well have been left unsaid. David knew that there was a time for speaking and another for silence, so he turned away from Eliab. It cannot have been an easy thing to do. All of us love to justify ourselves before men. We have a strong natural urge to put ourselves in the right, but it is often best quietly to turn away in the moment when we are reviled. So young David achieved a superb victory in that quiet corner of the battlefield. He left the angry Eliab and moved off to talk with others.

2 VICTORY OVER THE FLESH—*the meeting with Saul* (*1 Sam. 17:31-39*)

David had successfully overcome his natural inclination to answer his brother back; now he is made to enter the warfare again. The Enemy is subtle and this temptation is not quite so obvious. Any godly man knows that hasty speech is best answered by silence. "A soft answer turneth away wrath" (Prov. 15:1). But now the scene changes and, with it, the temptation. When we are victorious in one realm, the Devil will see to it that we are quickly confronted with a different kind of temptation. He does his utmost to catch us when we are off our guard. This time, David was in the presence of the king himself. It soon came to the ears of Saul that there was a man in the ranks who was not afraid of Goliath. Once he was brought into the king's presence, young David made his formal offer of service. He was not amongst Saul's enrolled soldiers but he made it clear to the king that he was prepared to be a volunteer. "Let no man's heart fail because of him; thy servant will go and fight with this Philistine"(17:32). Saul reminded David of Goliath's skill in the art of warfare. "He has been fighting battles ever since he was your age," says Saul. "There's a whole lifetime of experience behind the man." But David begged the king to let him go. Saul listened to an honest account of David's conquests over the wild animals which had often attacked his father's sheep in the wilderness and, in the end, he consented. After all, what could be lost? The youth from Bethlehem could at least have a try and, if he lost, he would be but the first of many Israelites who might eventually be slain by the Philistine warrior.

Then David's second temptation presented itself. Saul moved over to the corner of the tent and proceeded to dress David up in the best armour that could be found in Israel—the king's own suit of mail. He must have looked a strange sight. The helmet of brass was secure on his head and the great coat of mail hung loosely around him. David himself put the belt around his waist and made sure that the magnificent royal sword was in its place and then "assayed to go" (17:39). Those three words paint a wonderful scene, not without its humour. The Revised Standard Version translates them "He tried in vain to go". All dressed up and ready for action, he tried to put his best foot forward but could hardly move a few inches. He knew that it was impossible to fight in those clothes, so he plucked up courage and told Saul that he could not possibly stride on to the battle-field dressed in the king's armour. "David put them off him" (17:39).

We cannot meet giants with their own weapons. The apostle Paul knew this. Remember what he said to the Corinthians: ". . . we do not war after the flesh: for the weapons of our warfare are not carnal, but mighty through God to the pulling down of strongholds" (2 Cor. 10:3f.). We cannot win our battles against the world by using the world's methods. God provides the man or woman of faith with a different kind of armour, and there is an immense amount about it in the New Testament. Paul was particularly fascinated by the subject and mentioned it to several of the churches for which he had special concern (Rom. 13:12; 2 Cor. 6:7; Eph. 6:13ff.; 1 Thess. 5:8). We are not going to triumph by our self-confidence, or our rich experience. This is to rely on the "flesh"; this is to fight battles in the way the world tries to fight and it is doomed to failure. This was a

31

lesson David was quick to learn that day as he stood in Saul's tent. The king's heavy armour was put to one side and he went out into the bright sunshine trusting utterly and completely in the God who had promised to help His people.

3 VICTORY OVER THE GIANT—*the meeting with Goliath* (*1 Sam. 17:40-54*)
The young warrior had two important victories behind him. The third now became a glorious possibility. How did David conquer Goliath that day? The narrative reveals a number of important truths which are of equal importance to us as we engage in the good fight of faith. The Christian life has been rightly likened to a battle. There are glorious conquests to be won and great victories to be obtained. All too often, like Saul and his fearful soldiers, we tremble with fear but, now and again, God thrusts forth a "David" who stirs us all to greater reliance. To the man who is weak in faith, those memorable lines in Ibsen's *Brand* come as a sharp rebuke:

> *My God is of another mind—*
> *A storm, where yours is but a wind:*
> *Where yours is deaf, inexorable:*
> *All-loving, where your God is dull.*
> *And He is young, like Hercules—*
> *No grandad in the seventies.*
> *His voice in awful thunders rolled*
> *What time the Thorn-bush flamed, of old,*
> *And shrank, on Horeb's trembling height,*
> *Ev'n Moses to a pigmy mite.*
> *He stayed the sun in Gibeon's vale,*
> *And other wonders, passing tale,*
> *He did, and even yet would do*
> *Were not the age grown slack, like you.*

How was David able to step out with such confidence on to that strange battle-field?
(a) He became confident *as he thought of the various times*

*when God had been his helper in the past* (1 Sam. 17:34-36). When you are fighting hard, and the battle is fierce and exhausting, think for a moment about the good hand of God upon you in the past, and you will prove how adequate is His strength for today. Years before David was born, but at an equally difficult time of testing for God's people, the prophet Samuel had raised a memorial stone to remind the Israelites of God's unfailing power. This also was during a period of Philistine oppression and they called the monument "Ebenezer"—the Stone of Help. The words on the stone have come down the centuries, receiving added testimony from thousands of other conquerors who have also proved their truth: "Hitherto hath the Lord helped us" (1 Sam. 7:12). Similarly, David knew that the God who had stood at his side as he fought with wild beasts would not let him down as he walked out to meet Goliath.

(b) But David knew that mere history would not save him. He walked out to meet the Philistine leader with *the deep assurance in his heart and mind that God was still eager to help him in his present difficulty*. At that moment he was not looking back; he was looking up. He rehearsed the account of God's help on the day he met the lion and the bear but went on to assert: "The Lord that delivered me . . . will deliver me out of the hand of this Philistine" (17:37). No amount of testimony about past blessings will get us through if we lack the certainty that He is sufficient for today. Faith must be brought up to date. We can be encouraged by yesterday's triumphs but we cannot live on them. The Christian life demands a constantly renewed sense of confidence in the God who is always the same.

(c) We turn now to a wonderfully practical note in the story. David left Saul's armour behind in the king's tent, but "he took his staff in his hand, and chose him five smooth stones out of the brook" (17:40). As we fight battles for the Lord, we have to be prepared *to bring our utmost by making use of those particular gifts He has given us*. David had proved God's might whilst he was a shepherd. He did not know much about military manoeuvres but he knew a good deal about what a shepherd would do in a similar difficulty, so he gave that to God. He stepped forth armed with a simple shepherd's outfit—staff, scrip, stones and sling (17:40). It must have seemed so ridiculous to the terror-stricken on-lookers, but in the use of these simple things David was immensely gifted and those skilful hands were strengthened by God. We often fail in time of temptation because we are not prepared to bring our utmost in faith, prayer, sincerity, sacrifice and dependence.

(d) David needed something more: *a complete reliance on the God who promises to deliver*. He was willing for those simple shepherd skills to be used by God, but he was not trusting solely in them. His faith was in the God who had fought His people's battles for centuries. The Israelite soldiers had forgotten that Jehovah was "the Lord of hosts", an expression which can be translated "God of the battalions of Israel". Goliath was offended at David's staff, so David made fun of Goliath's sword, shield and spear. He knew that the giant was relying on these three pieces of equipment so he told the Philistine where he was putting his trust—not in a few military weapons but "in the name of the Lord of hosts, the God of the armies of Israel". The lad from Bethlehem knew full well that he could not hope to do it in his own energy; only God could do it through him. His trust was in God and his cry of confidence rang through the valley: "The battle is the Lord's and He will give you into our hands" (17:47).

(e) David's motive in all this is extremely important. *He was concerned about the honour of God's Name*. He was not anxious for a victorious consequence so that the king could continue his sad reign in peace. The peace of men was hardly in his mind at all. He had a greater concern—the glory of God. He *had* to win so that all that assembled host would know that his God did not save by swords and spears but by His own mighty arm (17:47). David knew that if Goliath were to win the battle the name of Jehovah would be ridiculed throughout every Philistine town and village. Does this question of God's glory matter to us? In our troubles, people are looking on, waiting to see what will happen. Great Christians have fought before us and by their conquests have brought glory to God. Now we are presented with our opportunity. If we remember that God's honour is at stake, and resolve only to work and fight for His glory, we too will share David's victory.

(f) There is one thing more. David looked along the valley towards Goliath and started to run. As he gathered speed, one prayer ran through his mind. It was that God would be true to His promise and *give him the necessary power at precisely the right moment*. The man who wants to use a sling has to be fairly near. It needed courage to run over the fields towards the monster but run he did, and then feeling in his bag for the stone, he slipped it into his sling, swirled it round and sent it soaring through the air. God's mighty power was behind that little stone. That's how to kill giants! With all the energy you have but with immense trust in the God who is able to do exceedingly abundantly above all that you can ask or think. Dr. Graham Scroggie used to say that it took Goliath completely by surprise; such a thing had never entered his head before!

Now we are on the battlefield. Time and again, fearful and totally unexpected giants come striding across our path and our first inclination is to run away, to protest that this particular fight is too hard or that God has been unfair to give us such an unusually difficult task to perform. But such a moment is our magnificent opportunity. Think about David at Elah and remember that the battle is the Lord's.

# 4

# THE SHEPHERD MEETS A ROYAL FAMILY

The biblical account of David's life continuously provides us with a rapid change of scene. We now move from the battle-field at Elah to the court of Saul. In 1 Samuel chapter 18 we are presented with a vivid description of three members of the royal house of Israel. First of all, the young shepherd from Bethlehem becomes friendly with Jonathan, the prince, then he has an encounter with Saul, the king, and finally meets Michal, the king's daughter. He has quite a different relationship with each of them and this passage from the Old Testament might well be entitled "a chapter in the study of relationships". There are clear illustrations here of totally different types of people whom we might well choose for our own friends. Someone has said, "a man is not the whole of himself; his friends are half of him." In other words, our friends help to make us what we are. Bad friends can mar our lives and good friends can be such an enrichment. Let us relate these stories to our own experience and think carefully about the people we have chosen for our friends.

## 1 THE FRIEND WHO BECAME A PROTECTOR

We turn first to David's friendship wih Jonathan, prince in Israel and natural heir to the throne. When the king died, men would certainly look to him as Saul's successor. He possessed charm and dignity, courage and skill, and the people at court would rest content about the future in the assurance that one day Jonathan would reign over them. But as the weeks went by Jonathan could see that David's victory over Goliath had turned the tide in the affairs of national leadership. The hearts of the people were going after David and he ultimately realized that he would not be king because of David, yet he still treasured and fostered the deep friendship that had grown up between them. In these few verses, we find a moving account of an enriching companionship.

(a) Consider first of all, *Jonathan's admiration*. He admired David's valour. Jonathan had trembled with the rest at the thought of meeting Goliath and, like all the other warriors at Saul's court, his heart was filled with admiration at the recollection of what happened that day as the young shepherd went running to meet the giant, naturally skilled yet absolutely reliant upon God, Jonathan also admired David's deep faith and rich devotion to the cause of God: "the battle is the Lord's, and he will give you into our hands" (17-47). Everyone else on the battlefield was terror-stricken but David's heart was full of peace, confidence and joyful assurance. He had spiritual qualities that his new friend admired.

In our relationships, do we go out of our way to rejoice in the qualities and the gifts of our friends? If we were to be asked about other people we know at work, at church, in our neighbourhood, would we instinctively list their many virtues, or would we find it much easier to point out all their mistakes? There is a biblical principle enshrined here which is frequently overlooked. Look again at 1 Corinthians 13:4-7. The passage is familiar to us and we have become so enamoured with its literary beauty that we forget its practical emphasis. The apostle Paul writes about the sort of thing we should not single out in other people's lives. "Love," he says "thinketh no evil." We should not spend time discovering the things we think might be wrong in other people. "What is more," he says, "we must never rejoice in iniquity." We should let other people enrich our lives as we notice in them the things that are good, admirable and exemplary. This is one of the things that Jonathan teaches us. He looked at

David and loved him. Saul looked at David and was filled with jealousy but when Jonathan saw him he was filled with admiration. Do we look at people with the Jonathan spirit?

(b) There is another thing we ought to notice which is closely allied to this; it concerns *Jonathan's unselfishness*. It is beautifully illustrated in the way he admired David's valour. It is all the more remarkable when you realize that Jonathan was no mean soldier himself. This battle with the giant, Goliath, is so well known that we tend to forget about some other courageous conflicts which were almost as remarkable. Jonathan was engaged in one which we can read about in 1 Samuel 14:1-16. The passage tells the story of how, when the nation was in serious difficulty, Jonathan went out, accompanied only by his armour-bearer, and the two of them slew an astonishing number of Philistine soldiers (1 Sam. 14-13). Jonathan had also been victorious in battle and yet, as he witnessed the people's acclamation and excitement, there was not a scrap of jealousy in his heart. He did not think for a moment about his own lack of prestige; he rejoiced in David's popularity. Do we rejoice when we hear of the success of other people? Or is our witness marred by the same jealous spirit as Saul's on the day when David was praised by the exultant women? John the Baptist is a wonderful New Testament illustration of the kind of joyful resignation and humility which God expects of us. He was a man who gathered a vast congregation and held hundreds of people in Judaea absolutely spellbound; and then watched this vast crowd slowly turning from him to follow Somebody else. But John the Baptist did not distress himself about it. His attitude is beautifully summarized in his deep conviction: "He must increase, but I must decrease" (John 3:30). He rejoiced in the greater popularity of Jesus. F. B. Meyer loved to tell the story of what happened on one of his frequent visits to the Northfield Convention in America. He had been a regular speaker for several years and held vast crowds spellbound with his fine expository gifts. Then one year a young preacher came along, of whom hardly anyone there had heard. His name was Campbell Morgan and, after hearing the new preacher, hundreds of the Convention visitors stopped going to Meyer's meetings and went instead to hear this brilliant new Bible teacher. Later on in his life, Meyer freely and openly confessed that he had a battle that week and the only way he won through to peace and abiding victory was by praying for Campbell Morgan every single day and at every possible opportunity in the day. In this way he was kept entirely free from any suggestion of rivalry or jealousy. He simply rejoiced that people were eager to hear the word of God; after all, the name of the preacher did not matter.

(c) There is something else to point out here: *Jonathan's generosity*. His action when he met David makes it abundantly clear that he did not only talk about his affection; he showed it by his spontaneous generosity. His devotion was not limited to a few well chosen words. "Jonathan stripped himself of the robe that was upon him and gave it to David" (1 Sam. 18-4). The action probably suggested that he was marking David out as a prince in Israel. In other words, when Jonathan had finished adorning David, he stood clothed as an ordinary man in Israel. When he took off his armour, he surrendered his life and his loyalty. What magnificent parallels there are in this passage both to our relationship with the Lord and to each other. We should be so thrilled by Christ's coming to this world and His victory on our behalf, that we have offered Him the "garments" of our distinctive personality and surrendered our lives, our swords, our skills, our all into His hands. Jonathan honoured David in this intensely moving and essentially practical way. What a magnificent beginning for a friendship.

## 2 THE FRIEND WHO BECAME AN OPPONENT

Now to something less pleasing, found in 1 Samuel 18:5-16. Here David meets the king at court. It is in this passage of Scripture that we first observe Saul's bitter jealousy and rivalry: "It came to pass as they came, when David was returned from the slaughter of the Philistine, that the women came out of all cities of Israel singing and dancing to meet King Saul, with tabrets, with joy, and with instruments of musick. And the women answered one another as they played, and said, Saul hath slain his thousands and David his ten thousands. And Saul was very wroth, and the saying displeased him: and he said, They have ascribed unto David ten thousands, and to me they have ascribed but thousands: and what can he have more but the kingdom? And Saul eyed David from that day and forward." Jealousy distorts our judgment and corrupts our thinking. It comes out in cruel speech, bitter attitudes and ugly resentments. There are some strong words about it in the Old Testament and we would do well to remind ourselves of them. *Proverbs* speaks about the restless torment that goes on in the mind of a jealous man—"For jealousy is the rage of a man; therefore he will not spare in the day of vengeance. He will not regard any ransom; neither will he rest content, though thou givest many gifts" (Prov. 6:34-35). The leading character in Shakespeare's *Othello* is a good and guileless man who has no reason at all to be jealous. His wife is the most loyal and loving person imaginable, but Othello becomes manipulated by a rascal. Seeds of bitter jealousy are sown in his mind by his evil friend, and before long innocent events are viewed with deep anguish and in bitter suspicion. The whole thing ends in terrible grief; one tragedy is heaped upon another and it all started with jealousy. Jealousy is a sin that will quickly spawn a series of other dreadful evils. If only King Saul could have conquered it: but it burned vehemently in his heart like a raging fire, and made it quite impossible for him to see David's fine qualities. This is another dreadful thing about jealousy: it mars our vision. It blinds us to good and lovely things in other people's lives. David had many qualities which Jonathan obviously saw and admired, but Saul was quite unable to see them. All these virtues would have enriched Saul's life. We lose so much spiritual blessing when we fail to notice the good things in other people.

Here are four things which Saul failed to see in David because he was so jealous of him:

(a) First of all, there was *David's unbounded affection*. He had an overflowing love for men which was genuine and sincere. In 1 Samuel 18 there are several references to David's love and it reminds us that the person who is loving towards other people receives love himself. Verse 5, for example, says "And David went out whithersoever Saul sent him, and behaved himself wisely: and Saul set him over the men of war, *and he was accepted in the sight of all the people*, and also in the sight of Saul's servants." Verse 16: "But all Israel and Judah loved David because he went out and came in before them." He did not change his friends because he had got in with the royal family; he moved among ordinary people with deep gratitude for their friendship and affection. But Saul did not see that. His tormented mind dwelt on the possibility that this young upstart might steal his kingdom.

(b) Then there was *David's spiritual wisdom*: this could also have been a great blessing to Saul but he was far too consumed with rivalry and bitterness to notice it. There are several references in this chapter to David's wisdom and discretion (vv. 5, 14-15, 30). "David behaved himself more wisely than all the servants of Saul; so that his name was much set by." If only Saul had learnt from this. The New Testament asserts that wisdom is a gift of God (Jas. 1:5).

(c) Then we must also notice *David's deep humility*. The young warrior had been promised that, as he was successful in battle, he could marry Saul's elder daughter, but David said to Saul: "Who am I? and what is my life, or my father's family in Israel, that I should be son in law to the king?" (1 Sam. 18:18, cf. 18:23). It is a clear example of his genuine self-effacement. These were rich qualities which Saul was not able to see and appreciate because he was so terribly jealous of David.

(d) Finally, Saul was not able to appreciate *David's close companionship with God.* Verse 12 says "Saul was afraid of David, because the Lord was with him," and verse 28: "Saul saw and knew that the Lord was with David." Remember some years earlier Saul had possessed these blessings himself.

## 3 THE FRIEND WHO BECAME A SNARE

Saul tried to destroy David, first by outward enemies, the Philistines (1 Sam. 18:17), and then when that failed, he planned to destroy him by an inward foe—someone really close to him. This brings us to the third friend we meet in this chapter, Saul's daughter, Michal. Saul said, "I will give him her, that she may be a snare to him, and that the hand of the Philistines may be against him." Saul knew that there were two ways he might destroy this man, either out on the battle-field or in his own house. He knew his daughter well enough to know that she could probably ruin David if she set her mind to it. She did not ruin him, in fact, but did cause David immense grief of heart and mind because she did not love the Lord God as he did. Michal seemed to love David at first, but Saul knew her well enough to know that she would not do him any good. In marrying her, David obviously made an awful mistake. He was so warm and friendly but, despite his discretion in other matters, perhaps he was not as wise in this as he ought to have been. On his wedding day, this devout youth was welcoming serious trouble to his heart and home. This matter of forming close relationships with people who do not love the Lord is such a serious one. All of us must be genuinely friendly towards those who do not share our faith but those bonds of strong affection which lead to the closest possible union should be reserved for our fellow Christians. There is a well-known passage about this: "Be ye not unequally yoked together with unbelievers: for what fellowship hath righteousness with unrighteousness? and what communion hath light with darkness?" (2 Cor. 6:14). God's Word asserts that we must not form a really close relationship with someone who does

42

not love the Lord. The best partner for a Christian is one who shares his faith and loyalty.

Before we leave this study in relationships we note one final thing: no man is ever free from the possibility of sinning. Saul sent David to battle in the hope that some Philistine soldier would kill him: "Let the hand of the Philistines be upon him . . . But Saul thought to make David fall by the hand of the Philistines" (1 Sam. 18:17, 25). It was a grim thing to do. But, later in his life, David did exactly the same thing when he wanted to get rid of a man (2 Sam. 11:14ff.). Once again we recall Paul's words: "Wherefore let him that thinketh he standeth take heed lest he fall" (1 Cor. 10:12).

# 5

# ONLY A STEP FROM DEATH

The passages for our study in this chapter are those found in
1 Samuel chapters 19 to 21. These narratives form a unity
and even suggest a common theme. They present a study in
"God's protecting grace". The theme is that of the kindly
providence of God. By this time David was in great need.
Obviously, Saul was mentally disturbed. The longing to get
rid of David had become tragically obsessional. "And Saul
was yet the more afraid of David; and Saul became David's
enemy continually" (18:29). The only thought which
pounded through Saul's mind at this time was that David's
popularity might rob him of prestige, influence and power.
As the women rejoiced over David's victories (18:6f.) and
joined in that careless song about David's excellence, Saul's
heart began to fret: "What can he have more but the kingdom?" (18:8). Yet David was the last man Saul needed to
fear. The young man's rich qualities and devotion were
obvious to everyone, but it is not easy to quieten a deeply
troubled mind.

Saul was not only afraid of David; he was jealous of him
too. Saul was a warrior and would love to have had the
slaughter of Goliath to his credit. Fear had robbed him of
that victory. In the days when he was spiritually loyal he
would have walked into the valley of Elah and met a team of
giants, but it was different now. He kept thinking of
David's resounding victory and, whenever it crossed his disturbed mind, the words of the thoughtless women set his
fears to discordant music: "Saul hath slain his thousands and
David his ten thousands" (18:7). How different Saul and his
son were in this respect. Jonathan felt his heart leap for joy

when he saw young David return from the battlefield, exhausted and elated after the death of Goliath. But Saul's heart lay cold within him. Perhaps from this point on Saul began to feel terribly insecure. He knew deep down inside that he had been rejected from being king. The prophet Samuel had told him so in unmistakable terms (15:26); he had also said that God had given the kingdom to "a neighbour of thine that is better than thou" (15:28), and those words suited David perfectly. The fact that Jonathan had befriended the youth from Bethlehem only made matters worse. His son was devoted to David but perhaps his daughter would destroy him. When his anguish was at its worst he called Jonathan and his servants to his tent and demanded that David be sought and slain (19:1). That opening verse of our passage sets the dismal scene for three whole chapters. David's life was at stake, but he rejoiced in the truth that his destiny was not in the hands of Saul, but in the hand of God. Later in his life he gave rich expression to his faith in God's providential care and said, "If it had not been the Lord who was on our side, when men rose up against us: then they had swallowed us up quick . . . Blessed be the Lord, who hath not given us as a prey to their teeth" (Ps. 124:2f., 6). In the providence of God he was to be given a long and rewarding life, but he hardly knew that when Saul's troops were in daily pursuit. In those dark days, his rich faith sustained him, so that he could later share his secret: "When my heart is overwhelmed: lead me to the rock that is higher than I. For Thou hast been a shelter for me and a strong tower from the enemy" (Ps. 61:2f.).

Yet, although David had such strong faith and spiritual confidence, the Lord knew that he would need friends in his trouble and in this study we look at those who supported him in desperate circumstances. Chapters 19 to 21 of 1 Samuel introduce us to seven scenes in David's life during this dangerous period. He knew that day after day there was but a step between himself and death. He said so to his closest friend (1 Sam. 20:3) and nobody could deny it. As we look at those who were used to help him through these perilous experiences we are reminded that the Lord still uses ordinary human friends, as well as extraordinary events, to bring His children through adversity.

## 1 THE PRINCE WHO PLEADED DAVID'S CAUSE

The first scene set in the court of Saul is found in 1 Samuel 19:1-7. Jonathan is ordered to kill David but he is sure that a good deal of his father's anger can be skilfully averted so sets himself to talk quietly with the king about David's innocence. Jonathan is a wonderful example of the peacemaker. Some elements had to be introduced that Saul had not previously considered, and Jonathan dealt with it all quite positively by reminding his father of David's many qualities and the rich assets these virtues would bring to court.

The Prince talks to his father about *David's loyalty*. In his discussion with Saul he deliberately refers to David as Saul's "servant" (19:4). The king is sinning against one of his most loyal men. Jonathan is eager to make Saul aware of the truth that David is not at court as a cunning usurper, but as a devoted subject.

Jonathan makes a point of stressing *David's innocence*. He protests that it would be wrong for his father to "sin against his servant" because, as he puts it, "he hath not sinned against thee" (19:4). Perhaps David's pure life was a rebuke to Saul. When wilful sinners are confronted by a holy life, they tend to react against it violently and unjustly.

Jonathan tells Saul about *David's service*. He can speak quite positively about David. "His works have been to thee-ward very good" (19:4). Some of David's exploits on the king's behalf were known to everyone at court. To return this kindness by hunting him down was insane.

Jonathan's final point is to remind his father of *David's valour*. This may have been a risky thing to do, but he knew that David's bravery might well appeal to Saul: "For he did put his life in his hand and slew the Philistine, and the Lord wrought a great salvation for all Israel: thou sawest it, and didst rejoice: wherefore then wilt thou sin against innocent blood, to slay David without a cause?" (19:5). Jonathan reminds his father that at one time he was as delighted as anyone about David's courageous encounter with the Philistine leader. Perhaps his most skilful point was that of his reference to the Lord's use of David and its obvious benefit to "all Israel". By speaking positively about the fact that God was on David's side, he was calmly suggesting to his father that his action in pursuing David was likely to offend God, who had been pleased to use His servant as their national deliverer.

Saul listened carefully to his son as he calmly presented his arguments and changed his mind—but not his heart.

## 2 THE WOMAN WHO SAVED DAVID'S LIFE

David was reinstated in the king's favour and at this time the nation was again exposed to Philistine attack. "And there was war again: and David went out, and fought with the Philistines, and slew them with a great slaughter; and they fled from him" (19:8). After the victory, Saul's jealous spirit got the better of him once again. What a strange mixture he was. H. G. Wells says of one of his characters in *The History of Mr. Polly*: "He was not so much a human being as a civil war." This is an apt description of Saul. His mind was deeply disturbed; his spirit was not at peace with God and therefore he could not hope to be one with his fellows. An incident occurred as David was playing his harp at court. In a moment of rising fury, Saul hurled his javelin at his musician, and all the old trouble flared up again. The expert soldier was a gifted musician, and in times past he had calmed Saul's tumultuous spirit by his restful songs. What a difference between the two men—David with his harp and Saul with his javelin. Do we have a quiet, restorative, healing effect on those in our company, or are we more likely to use the javelin? David was eager to enrich life whilst Saul was determined to destroy it.

The same night David rushed home in order to escape.

Psalm 59 indicates that, in these grim moments, David turned to prayer. The title dates this majestic song at a time "when Saul sent, and they watched the house to kill him". It is a moving plea for deliverance. David was aware that blood-thirsty men were around every corner lying in wait for his soul (Ps. 59:2f.) but he knew of a God who was intent on his protection: "The God of my mercy shall prevent me" or "go before me" (59:10). The Revised Standard Version says "My God in his steadfast love will meet me." In this he found confidence and peace. At this critical time in his life the Lord knew He could use Michal, David's wife, to bring him to safety. As David was let down from a window, Michal put her own life in jeopardy by keeping the soldiers at bay pretending that her husband was ill. When Saul's men eventually came into the house to kill David they found that they had been deceived. One of the most revealing things about the story is the detail about the image Michal put in the bed. It was a teraphim, an idol, directly forbidden by the law of Moses. Its very presence in her house says something about the poverty of her devotion to the Lord. "Teraphim" were of foreign importation and were generally held in derision (cf. Gen. 31:19ff., Judges 17:5ff.) but Michal obviously had scant repect for God's law. The Word of God said that no Hebrew household should bow down and worship "any graven image", or "likeness of anything" (Exod. 20:4, Lev. 26:1, Deut. 27:15) but these great truths seem to have meant little to her. But, at this time, God took her and used her to get his servant away to freedom. From this point on she steps from the story and only emerges years later when the ark is brought back to Jerusalem. God is sovereign. In His glorious purposes for the believer He is free to use anyone for the blessing and protection of His people.

### 3 THE PROPHET WHO STRENGTHENED DAVID'S HEART

"So David fled, and escaped, and came to Samuel to Ramah, and told him all that Saul had done to him. And he and Samuel went and dwelt in Naioth" (19:18). The young man knew that in trouble he could turn to Samuel for sympathy, encouragement and advice. There is a word here for elderly people who are sometimes tempted to think that there is nothing left for them to do. The fact that any of us are still here on this earth is a sign that God has important work for us to do. Once our task is complete we shall go to be with Christ "which is far better". Our continuing life is a sign of God's claim upon our unfinished service. There is a real ministry for the elderly in every church. Two great things stand out about Samuel in this single verse.

(a) The first is that of *Samuel's approachability*. David realized that he could count on Samuel for good, sound advice. He would help him to discern the next step for his life. On the one hand, God had, almost secretly, marked him out as Saul's successor. On the other, the king was determined that he should never come to the throne. What was his future? Only Samuel could help him to see his way through these mists of perplexing uncertainty. Samuel was a very old man by now (1 Sam. 12:2) David's arrival at his home might easily have alarmed him. Anyone giving refuge to a man who was Saul's enemy immediately put his own life in serious danger. But David knew that Samuel would offer him both shelter and welcome. Do our friends have that kind of confidence in our love and generosity?

(b) The other quality is that of *Samuel's self-sacrifice*. The old prophet knew exactly how Saul's mind would work. It would soon get back to the court that David was at Ramah and the king's soldiers would be in quick pursuit. Samuel did not send David on somewhere else. He felt it best to stay by him as his counsellor and spiritual father, so both of them left Ramah for Naioth. It was a marvellous thing for an old man to do. He had known many difficult years of leadership and responsibility, and could be excused if he now wished to enjoy the quietness of Ramah. But he knew that he had to accompany David. It is a wonderful thing when a Christian accepts a continuing responsibility for someone in need. Lots of people are prepared to do the occasional thing to

49

cheer a friend in adversity, but few are willing for the discipline and self-sacrifice of regular help. One of the attractive things about the Samaritan in Christ's famous parable is that he was not content just to bind up the victim's wounds and take him to a place of safety. He accepted a greater responsibility by paying for all the charges at the inn until the man had fully recovered (Luke 10:35). He was fully prepared to go "the second mile" (cf. Matt. 5:41) without any kind of pressure other than the compulsion of love. Samuel had that same desire and so he left the comfort and peace of his home preferring to be a fugitive with David than to stay in peaceful Ramah whilst God's young servant wandered in danger.

## 4 THE SPIRIT WHO BAFFLED DAVID'S ENEMIES

We have already seen how God can use different types of people to help a believer in need. Our next scene portrays God's Holy Spirit in direct action on David's behalf. Sometimes God chooses to act through friends and acquaintances, using them as the instruments of His purpose. But at other times He directly intervenes by His miraculous power, and this scene unfolds such an encounter (1 Sam. 19:19-24).

It was inevitable that Saul and his spies would eventually find Samuel and the fugitive, and the day arrived when the prophet and his friend found themselves surrounded by the king's messengers. It looks as though they had found temporary refuge with a group of wandering prophets, some of whom were given to the practice of ecstatic utterance. The phenomenon was reasonably common throughout the ancient near east (Num. 11:25) and was often regarded as an indication of divine power. No sooner had the king's soldiers closed in upon the group than they felt themselves under the spell of this overwhelming power. They felt as though they had lost all control of their faculties and one moment they were swaying in ecstasy and the next grovelling in fear. The message soon got back to Saul that his soldiers had not successfully completed their mission and he quickly dispatched a second contingent to make the arrest. They too became dominated by this strange power, and exactly the same happened to a third party. Enraged by these bewildering events, Saul determined to make the arrest himself. But, as soon as he came near to the wanted men, the Spirit of God invaded his mind and body. Tearing at his garments, he lost all control of speech and action and as the king broke out in ecstatic utterances, Samuel and David fled away for safety.

How wonderful that the Holy Spirit should undertake for His two servants in such a miraculous way. God had sent one person after another to help David in his trouble, but now he was beyond all human aid; only a miraculous intervention could free him from his oppressors, so God sent His Spirit. The Spirit of God is sometimes known as "the Paraclete"; the word means "one called alongside to help". He was certainly David's helper that day at Naioth. His ministry in our lives during adversity may not be so spectacular and dramatic, but it is just as real and gives us daily strength. The Early Christians certainly proved the Spirit's power in those difficult days at the beginning of the Church's history. Another Saul was pursuing them, rushing from house to house to make arrests and create havoc. But he too was overwhelmed by the Spirit of God, changed by the Living Christ, and transformed into the missionary-hero of the New Testament.

## 5 THE FRIEND WHO VALUED DAVID'S LOVE

David longed to see his friend Jonathan again. Chapter 20 sets the next scene. The detailed narrative in this chapter provides us with further insights into Jonathan's heart and mind and covers four important realms—spiritual, domestic, national and personal.

### (a) Jonathan's devotion to his God

Jonathan took an oath before the Lord (20:12f.) which tells us a good deal about his love for God. Saul had made promises and invoked the assistance of the Divine Name, but they were mere words. He had clearly said "As the Lord liveth, he shall not be slain" but within days of his oath he had hurled his own javelin at David. His word was not to be trusted and the fact that he introduced God's name into his promises meant nothing. Other people knew only too well that he did not honour the God upon whom he called. But when Jonathan mentioned God's name it was in the spirit of reverence and awe. He refused to use God's name in a dishonouring way. It meant far too much to him. It is not only what we *say* about God that matters. It is what we *are* that counts.

### (b) Jonathan's devotion to his family

He was rightly concerned about the welfare of his children in the event of his death, and asked David to promise that he would have his children's needs at heart should anything happen to him: "also thou shalt not cut off thy kindness from my house for ever" (20:15). Jonathan knew only too well that the day was coming when David would sit on the throne of Israel. He wanted to be sure that his family would be safe at such a time and it was typical of him to look out into the distant future and make plans for their safe keeping David was ready to make his friend such a promise and, as we shall see later, just as eager to keep it (2 Sam. 2:9).

### (c) Jonathan's devotion to his nation

As he pledged his loyalty to David, he knew that his friend was God's appointed ruler over Israel. He realized how much his father had grieved God and was relieved to know that one day his people would be in better hands. It was this quiet resignation to what Jonathan knew to be God's will that made his father so furious. In a wild rage Saul cried out to him: "For as long as the son of Jesse liveth upon the ground, thou shalt not be established, nor thy kingdom. Wherefore now send and fetch him unto me, for he shall surely die" (20:31). Jonathan refused to obey his father for he knew that the good hand of God was upon David. He was not interested in self-exaltation and only wanted to do what was right before God. He knew what havoc had been brought into Saul's life through spiritual rebellion, self-seeking and disobedience, and he had no desire to follow in his father's steps.

### (d) Jonathan's devotion to his friend

He risked his life for David. Once again Saul demanded David's death, but the prince put in a further plea for him and protested his friend's innocence: "Wherefore shall he be slain? what hath he done?" It was a comment which almost cost him his life (20:32f.). Loyal friends were in short supply at his father's court. Everyone feared Saul and, for the sake of their own lives, were prepared to please the king by killing his enemy, innocent though he might be. David could not count on many friends in that circle, but Jonathan was worth a score of Saul's time-servers.

As a good son Jonathan must often have prayed that his father's troubled spirit would be calmed. It says much for his love for his father that he was still eager to plead with Saul rather than be angry with him. But David knew how desperately the king longed for his death, and so the two friends planned a scheme whereby Saul's feelings about David might be put to a final test. At the special festivals of the year, all the princes were expected to dine at court. David realized that it was a breach of etiquette for him not to be in his place but he knew that if Saul had overcome his jealousy and bitterness he would not resent his absence. Saul's reaction on seeing the empty seat would indicate something of his present feelings. All that remained was to plan carefully a means of communicating the news of Saul's attitude to David. The friends thought it best to do it whilst Jonathan was engaged in archery practice. If David hid in a certain spot and Jonathan shot his arrows alongside the hiding-place, David would know that it was all right to come before the king again. If the arrows reached well beyond the place where David was hidden, the fugitive would know that he must get well beyond Saul's court if he wanted to remain alive. David's worst fears were quickly realized. Saul was furious at his absence from the court festival and, angry at his son's continuing loyalty to David, hurled his javelin across the room "whereby Jonathan knew that it was determined of his father to slay David" (20:33). The following morning, Jonathan went out to the field with his boy servant and, at the appointed time, directed the arrow well beyond the place where his friend was hiding. David knew from that moment that it was no longer safe for him to stay anywhere near Saul's court. Jonathan's instructions to the lad sounded clearly over the fields: "Make speed, haste, stay not." David knew it to be the warning word of his best friend. In the moment that followed he also realized how costly it was for Jonathan to send him away. It has become one of the most moving scenes in the whole of the Old Testament. The agony of parting was only made bearable because of their deep conviction that the Lord would always stand between them (20:42) joining them together in a bond of unchanging loyalty and trust.

## 6 THE PRIEST WHO SUPPLIED DAVID'S NEEDS

In the scene that follows David made his way to a priestly sanctuary at Nob (1 Sam. 21:1-9). He arrived at the home of the priest Ahimelech tired and hungry. Jonathan's warning words, shouted across the fields, were still ringing in his ears: "Make speed, haste, stay not." He knew that it would not be long before Saul's troops would be combing the surrounding countryside, and in the cities and villages there would be plenty of people who would act as the king's spies.

When David came to the little community at Nob, he felt sure that the priests and their families would help him on his way. But possibly by this time the people were becoming aware of the king's bitterness. It was no longer something

secretly discussed in court circles; the ordinary folk in Israel were getting to know that David's popularity had become a threat to the king. Ahimelech was hesitant, if not fearful, when David arrived without the bodyguard which usually accompanied him; perhaps the courtier was in trouble after all. David badly needed food and had to get on his way so he told Ahimelech that he was on a secret mission from Saul and requested five loaves of bread. There was no ordinary bread available at that moment but it was the Sabbath day and, under certain conditions, the priest was allowed to give the holy shewbread which had just been removed from the table. This bread was really meant for priests but Ahimelech obviously believed it right to share it with a man in need provided that he purified himself in eating it in the same manner as the priests. His actions were certainly approved by God for the Lord Jesus reminded the Pharisees of the story on another Sabbath when men were hungry (Mark 2:26). How astonished that priest would have been had he known that centuries later his kind action would be mentioned with warm approval by the Messiah Himself. We do not know the ultimate blessing which can come through genuine sacrificial service. The woman who broke the alabaster box of ointment in the presence of Christ, using her hair as a towel, would never have dreamed it possible that wherever men preached the good news in later centuries her adoring act would be mentioned with thanksgiving and gratitude.

David did not only want food, however, he needed a sword, and in answer to his further request Ahimelech gave him the special trophy they kept in the sanctuary at Nob. This was the sword which David had taken from Goliath on the battlefield at Elah. David then departed. An Edomite herdsman employed by Saul had noticed their acts of kindness but the priests had no reason to fear his presence in the encampment. They could never have realized how tragic it was that this foreigner had been a witness. It was to bring untold grief to the whole community.

In the three chapters with which we are concerned in this study (1 Sam: 19–21) we have met a group of people who were used to help David when he was only a step from death. In one particular scene, when no human aid would suffice, the Holy Spirit Himself directly intervened. In our final scene David is caught in another difficult situation where no man could help him, but he cried to God who quickly provided him with an immediate solution to his problem (1 Sam. 21:10-15). David realized that he was not safe anywhere in Israel. He was compelled to seek refuge outside the borders of Israel and so he cast himself upon the mercy of a Philistine king, Achish of Gath. But his reputation as a military leader was known beyond the borders of Israel and the captains of Achish recognized him. David began to wonder whether he had done the right thing. Fear robbed him of his sleep and he tried to think out a way of escape. The title to Psalm 34 indicates that it belongs to this time and the psalm tells us that in this trouble he "sought the Lord" who heard him and delivered him from all his fears (Ps. 34:4). "This poor man cried, and the Lord heard him, and saved him out of all his troubles" (Ps. 34:6). He realized that God was sufficient, even in this very dark hour, and He would be David's redeemer. The psalm became a testimony to the great truth that "none of them that trust in Him shall be desolate" (Ps. 34:22). The answer was given to his prayer. Madmen were feared in the ancient near east. There was something uncontrollable and unpredictable about them. They reminded the onlooker of the weird, the inexplicable and the dangerous. No eastern court would give continuing hospitality to a mentally sick man and so David feigned madness, and it worked. The Philistines took him out through the gates of Gath, glad to be relieved of this pathetic lunatic. David was equally glad to be away from the city but a day was to come when, in greater danger still, he would be equally glad to return.

Psalm 34 should be read with this incident in mind. The

bewildered fugitive slept by day and walked by night. He heard the roar of hungry lions but the events of the days that followed convinced him of the truth that "they that seek the Lord shall not want any good thing" (Ps. 34:10). It was all right to sing "I shall not want" on the hills of Bethlehem; in those days there was father, brothers, friends and home. Now, humanly speaking, there was nothing—but God was with him, and that was enough.

# 6

# AND ALL BECAUSE OF AN
# INNOCENT SONG!

We turn now to 1 Samuel 22. By this time Saul's jealousy is at fever heat; David must be destroyed. These contrasting figures stand before us in Holy Scripture as a dreadful warning. When a man or woman becomes indifferent to the voice of God tragic things can happen. Selfish desires and the casual sayings or criticisms of friends will assume a far greater inportance than they deserve. It was so with Saul. Had he been in touch with God, the success of David would have encouraged him. He would have rejoiced that, at a critical time in the nation's life, a valiant man had been raised up by God to lead His people to freedom from the Philistine oppression. What is more, when the victor returned from the battle-field of Elah, he would not have resented the excited welcome of the Israelite women. There is not a hint of Saul's jealousy until that moment when the song was sung by the women in the streets (1 Sam. 18:6f.). Perhaps *they* were out of touch with God as well. They may have thought how superior a warrior David was, but there is no need to say everything that comes into our minds. Perhaps they were at fault in putting their thoughts into song. As the king heard their gay music, bitter jealousy rose up in his heart: "And Saul eyed David from that day and forward" (18:9). Possibly the women did not mean any harm by it. They were naturally excited but they were pathetically thoughtless. We often excuse ourselves a little too easily by saying "I did not mean any harm by it" as if that is supposed

to free us from all blame. Blameless motives do not necessarily free us from the charge of carelessness. We must think before we act and speak. Had the women sung in private, the subsequent trouble might never have happened in quite the way it did. But they danced in the presence of a man who was noticeably sensitive, spiritually weak and not a little moody (16:23). The words of the song were obviously true; their motives may have been absolutely pure, but their action was quite unwise. There is a time when it is right to speak and also a time when it is best to be silent (Eccles. 3:7).

We shall frequently see that one of the really frightening things about sin is its power to reproduce itself. This chapter (1 Sam. 22) is a stark illustration of this serious biblical theme. Saul's jealousy soon begets other sins. Our transgressions are never lonely: they rapidly give birth to others. A destructive process is set in motion whenever we sin and once it starts on its cruel mission we can do little to control it. In this study we look at five sins which followed hard on the heels of Saul's jealousy.

### 1 SELF PITY

Saul's bitterness towards David was like an infected wound. It poisoned his entire system. If he had been in close communion with God he would certainly have been able to conquer these overwhelming moods but he had cut himself off from the source of all help. In this kind of loneliness he turned his whole attention to himself and became obsessed with his own misfortunes and imaginary disasters. In reality, nobody was against him, but he mistrusted everyone. Note that this lack of confidence in others began in a wrong attitude to himself. When, like Saul, we dethrone God in our lives by our disobedience and rebellion, all inner harmony disappears. Self-pity is one of the sins which quickly rises to the surface in this sort of condition. What a tragic thing it is to see a person suffering from this sin. Surely we believe that our lives are in His hands. We can only feel sorry for ourselves by denying the reality of His providential care. If we are eaten up with self-pity, we are not believing the truth that "all things work together for good to them that love God, to them who are called according to His purpose" (Rom. 8:28). The "Saul" of the New Testament suffered through trials, persecutions, indignities and cruelties. Jews and Gentiles united in a common quest to mock him, arrest, whip, imprison, silence and, if possible, kill him. But never once did he say anything which carried the slightest suggestion of self-pity. Writing from a prison cell he could say "I have learned in whatsoever state I am, therewith to be content" (Phil. 4:11). In contrast Saul of the Old Testament was surrounded by wealth, comfort, loyal supporters and rich resources. But, haunted by an unnecessary fear, he looked at his courtiers and cried in pathetic self-pity: "there is none of you that is sorry for me" (1 Sam. 22:8). What a pitiful scene it must have been, this huge man, head and shoulders above everyone else, lamenting his hard lot! Self-pity robbed him of his dignity; it always does that. It ignores the mercy and compassion of God, believing human comfort and companionship to be of greater value.

## 2 SUSPICION

A further thing about self-pity is that it usually distorts facts. The lust for sympathy demands that the sense of tragedy be kept alive, intensified and, if possible, increased. Fresh causes of grief are constantly found so that there shall be no lack of sympathy from others. It is a subtle way of seeking attention and is so pathetically unchristian. Those who suffer from self-pity cannot assess their own life situation with any kind of accuracy. Innocent and harmless things are magnified into serious and offensive affronts and they are convinced that the whole world is against them. Saul was like that. He suspected everyone. He accused *Jonathan* of conspiracy and of actually inciting David to plot against him (22:8). There was not a grain of truth in it. Jonathan had constantly spoken of David's utter loyalty, and he meant it.

Saul also accused his *servants* of disloyalty. He was persuaded that they had access to information about this league of conspiracy and refused to share this knowledge with their king: "all you have conspired against me . . ." (22:8).

Even the *religious leaders* were not free from suspicion. The priests from Nob were summoned to the court and Saul screamed in wild rage at Ahimelech: "Why have ye conspired against me, thou and the son of Jesse . . . that he should rise against me, to lie in wait, as at this day?" (22:13). What a tragic scene it was. Ahimelech was as innocent as David and he, in turn, protested the loyalty of Jesse's son: "Who is so faithful among all thy servants as David, which is the king's son-in-law, and goeth at thy bidding, and is honourable in thine house?"

Saul's anger could not be assuaged, and yet all those who surrounded him at court that day were as innocent as his own son. Family, servants, priests, subjects, all are met by his accusing finger. Nothing could bring peace to their king's mind and the life of every man in Israel was imperilled if he so much as mentioned David's name. Saul kept on talking about David "lying in wait" (22:8,13). How easy it is to misrepresent a person's actions. David is hiding because of Saul's wrath. The king is persuaded that he is hiding in order to gather his rebellious army. The man who has lost his faith in God soon loses confidence in everyone else. It is a sad picture of a distorted mind and of the havoc and heartbreak it can bring to hundreds of others.

### 3 FALSEHOOD

The man who is disturbed in this way is never likely to be impressed by truth. Any information which supports or confirms his suspicion is certain to be received with gratitude. At this point we meet Doeg, the Edomite mule-keeper who had been present at Nob the day David was given food and a sword. He saw the occasion as an opportunity to ingratiate himself with the king but, not content to impart information, he added something to the story which was plainly untrue. He said that the priest in charge of the sanctuary "inquired of the Lord for him" (22:10). There was no truth in that statement, for had the priest been asked to discern God's mind about David's next step, his communion with God would obviously have revealed the serious nature of David's plight. Ahimelech thought that David was on a secret mission for Saul and had no idea that he was being pursued by the king's troops. Probably Doeg saw that David was engaged in serious conversation with Ahimelech and imagined that he was asking for the will of God to be revealed. Most of us have had some bitter experience of the same kind of thing. Some aggrieved soul jumps to conclusions about the subject of another person's conversation. They imagine from a casual glance that they are being discussed, and the grievance deepens. How important it is to know the *truth* when trying to assess a situation. On the other hand, Doeg may have known full well that they were only discussing the shewbread and manufactured the rest of the story to win a place in Saul's favour. He knew that the king was greedy for David's blood and that the death of David's friends would bring him temporary satisfaction.

This part of the story further illustrates the self-propagating power of sin. Doeg tells one untruth, and Saul in making his accusation to Ahimelech adds a further lie. He tells the priest that he has "inquired of God for him, *that he should rise against me, to lie in wait, as at this day*"(22:13). Now even Doeg did not go that far. He maintained that Ahimelech had "inquired of the Lord for him" but had not said anything about the answer the priest was supposed to have received. Such are the ways of sinners. One grief is added to another and the accusations become more and more unjust. This is what happens when men ignore the commandments of God. Doeg was an Edomite and had little regard for the law of Moses. Had he accepted such teaching he would have known that the God of Israel had clearly told this people that under no circumstances must they bear false witness against their neighbour (Exod. 20:16). Jehova was a God of Truth. His word was utterly dependable and he expected the same reliability of His children. Perhaps as an alien Doeg could be excused for his act, offensive as it was. But Saul was a Hebrew and he knew the Commandments as did all his fellow-countrymen. The law of God contained in *Deuteronomy* had serious things to say about the false witness (Deut. 19:16-20), but Saul cared nothing for God's Word. Doeg told the lie; but Saul loved it. Both belonged to the sad company of those who cut themselves off from grace because they do not care about truth.

## 4 MURDER

Ahimelech protests his innocence: "thy servant knew nothing of all this, less or more" (22:15), but Saul is determined to slay him. When one commandment is broken, it is easier to reject another. God's law also said "thou shalt not kill" (Exod 20:13) but Saul was deaf to the demands of God upon his life. He ordered his bodyguard to draw their swords and murder the priests, but they refused to do it. They knew them to be the anointed messengers of God. How wonderful that even among Saul's bodyguard there were those who remained true to God. Whilst the king was in such a vicious mood their disobedience could have cost them their lives, but they refused to stain their swords with innocent blood. Saul then turned to Doeg and ordered that he perform the execution. The Edomite saw this as a further opportunity to secure his popularity at court and gladly obeyed. What a dreadful scene—eighty-five innocent men cut down in a display of anger and fury—yet even more dreadful things were to happen.

Doeg's cruel mission was complete, but Saul's anger continued to rise and he demanded the life of every single person in Nob. Women and children were mercilessly slain and even their cattle were slaughtered. It was an act of vindictive cruelty in which nobody was spared. The place where the little priestly community had exercised their devout ministry was to become a perpetual reminder of the bitterness and hatred of Israel's first king. The blood of godly, loyal subjects ran in its streets and the Hebrew people were never to forget the dreadful crime. How could such a man, who could not control his own temper, continue to lead the nation? People's lives were in danger when they were anywhere near him. If an Edomite informer could cause the slaughter of hundreds of innocent people, who could be trusted and where was it all leading? Possibly Saul did it in a calculating kind of way to show what happened to anyone who dared even to speak to David. It was not only cruel; it was foolish. Sensible people began quietly to long for the day when David might assume the leadership of the nation. A maniac on the throne was hardly a comforting prospect, and thousands of devoted subjects secretly abandoned their allegiance and lived in hope of a better day. When the people heard about the tragic events at Nob, some of them might well have recalled Samuel's words about the greed of kings (1 Sam. 8:11ff). They knew that a king might take away their servants, but nobody could have dreamed that the first one would take away their lives. Samuel's warning came echoing over the years: "ye shall cry out in that day because of your king which ye shall have chosen you" (1 Sam. 8:18). Nobody would have believed that his sad words could have had such a speedy fulfilment.

As we have already observed, the tragedy was heightened by the fact that it need never have happened. The gay exuberant song of the careless women ended in the heartbreaking lament of hundreds in Israel. The man who in earlier days abounded in patience (10:26f.) and humility

64

(10:22f.) had become a raving lunatic and murderer. Once a man is out of touch with God, there is no limit to the harm and grief he can bring into the lives of others. Let this sad series of incidents remind us of the supreme importance of unbroken daily communion with God. Keep near to Him.

# 7

# PERSECUTED BUT NOT FORSAKEN

At this point in our study we turn to the narratives in 1 Samuel chapters 23 and 24. Paul's words about his own adversities (2 Cor. 4:9) provide a fitting title and remind us that in every century God's servants have been confronted with immense opposition but He has never left them or let them down. These chapters give us a vivid account of David's continuing hardships and are of spiritual importance to us in that they illustrate some of the rich qualities which characterize the true Christian in any period of testing.

We shall summarize the message of the chapters by looking first at David's *difficulties* and then at the secret of his *strength*.

1 DAVID'S DIFFICULTIES

Saul was not merely out to slay David but all his followers as well. The king was quite ready to cut down anybody who got in his way. David was obviously in hiding. His companions consisted of men who had lost hope, who were in distress, the debtors, the discontented, or as the margin puts it, those who were "in bitterness of soul". Men who had suffered any kind of anguish—these formed David's bodyguard of about four hundred men (1 Sam. 22:1-2). They were joined by Abiathar, the only priest to escape from Nob. He told David of the terrible slaughter of innocent men, women and children and, overwhelmed by grief, David bore all the responsibility for the disaster as he said: "I have occasioned the death of all the persons of thy father's house"

(22:22). But Saul's ferocity was not David's only trouble. He had to cope with serious problems in his own ranks.

(a) *Fear*. David was told that bands of Philistine marauders were making frequent attacks on the little town of Keilah, robbing them of their corn supplies. David asked the Lord whether he should fight these Philistine troops and God told him that he should. But David's four hundred men were terrified at the prospect. They said: "Behold, we be afraid here in Judah" (1 Sam. 23:3). "We are frightened if we stay where we are; after the massacre at Nob, it's dangerous enough to be in the region of Judaea without marching out into unknown enemy territory." There are few things more infectious than fear and we need to remind ourselves that the true Christian ought in every circumstance in life to endeavour to impart strength and fortitude to his friends, not fear. We live in a fear-ridden world. People are in fear and dread of financial failure, poor health, loneliness, loss of independence in old age, and a host of other things. There are those who are afraid of the future and others who are too fearful to face up to their present responsibilities in life. Many are afraid of death and refuse to think about the life to come. In a fearful society Christians have a glorious opportunity. Those who love Christ ought to be able to testify that "perfect love casteth out fear" (1 John 4:18). Like David we may encounter serious problems and grave difficulties but, with a deep confidence in God, we are adequate for every situation in life and we are encouraged to go on in faith believing in Him. Just before David's men had news of the Philistine raids on Keilah their spiritually-confident leader had said to Abiathar: "Stay with me, *fear not*; for he that seeks my life seeks your life; with me you shall be in safe-keeping" (1 Sam. 22:23 RSV). The committed Christian has that kind of assurance that if we are "in Christ" we too shall be in safe-keeping. When we think of David's men we may be tempted to think of them as fine, courageous stalwarts but many of them were not. He had fine soldiers to support him later, but at this time most of his men were afraid. There was a lot to terrify them of course. They were living in an unsettled country with a maniac on the throne. Abiathar had told them of the slaughter at Nob. Their wives and children were also in danger if they stayed with David. And now, he was suggesting that without proper arms they go to fight the Philistines!

(b) *Ingratitude*. Once David's men were assured that it was God's will for them to meet the Philistines (23:4-5) they went out to battle and conquered these oppressors. The citizens of Keilah rejoiced at the victory but Saul's spies soon informed him of David's whereabouts and before long the king's troops were making their way to Keilah to arrest him. Bewildered and uncertain about his next move, David further sought God's mind and asked the question whether the men of Keilah would hand him over to Saul (23:9-12). He was given the clear answer that, despite all he had done for that little town in the moment of its greatest need, the majority of its citizens would favour handing him over to Saul's soldiers. What appalling ingratitude! How sad it is when kindnesses are forgotten and people take some lovely thing for granted.

(c) *Treachery*. Saul had his spies everywhere and it was not even safe in the wilderness of Ziph. Some of the men who knew where he was hiding in those caves, sent to Saul and told him that they were prepared to lead the king to David's hide-out (23:19-24). David obviously did not expect opposition from this quarter. Trouble now seemed to be coming from every side. Fear in his own ranks, ingratitude from those he had risked his life to help, and now treachery from strangers. Life is like that sometimes; problems seem to come from every possible quarter. But David continued to trust in God.

(d) *Weakness*. By now David had six hundred men but Saul was soon to meet him with three thousand (24:2). Every single one of David's men knew that five of Saul's soldiers were after him. They were hopelessly outnumbered. David knew, however, that his strength was not in numbers. On the day when he went out to meet Goliath he had said that "the Lord saveth not with sword and spear" ( 1 Sam. 17:47). God is not dependent on large battalions. Throughout the centuries He has been pleased to use minorities to accomplish His mighty purposes (cf. 1 Cor. 1:27-29; Zech. 4:6).

## 2. DAVID'S STRENGTH

From where does a man get his strength, peace and resilience when he has to cope with such daunting trouble? There are four things here which should encourage every believer in times of adversity:

### (a) He sought God's will

David had a genuine desire to discover the purpose of God for every step of his life. Two incidents illustrate his concern in this matter (23:2 and 23:9-11). In both cases he "inquired of the Lord". Saul was not in the least bit interested in God's will; his only passion was to please himself and, in order to make sure that he did not hear the truth from God, he got rid of the people who were most likely to reveal it, the priests. Nobody could go to the sanctuary at Nob to "inquire of the Lord". The priests had been murdered, and it was the priests in Israel who sought God's mind. Men were told to seek instruction from them (Malachi 2:7). Unlike Saul, David wanted to know, so he went to a priest and he said to this only survivor of the slaughter of Nob: "Now, I want to know God's mind, Abiathar. Is it right for us to go to Keilah to help them?" The priest discerned God's will and said to David, "Go, and smite them." When David had obeyed that instruction he then asked the Lord, through Abiathar, whether he was going to be handed over to Saul by the inhabitants of the city, and whether it was right for him to leave it (23:9-12). He believed, of course, that "the steps of a good man are ordered by the Lord: and he delighteth in his way" (Ps. 37:23). The first thing that is characteristic of David is his passionate longing for God's will. This is of tremendous importance for all who are in trouble. The way to blessing is in a longing, not to escape from our adversity, but to discern the mind of God in it.

## (b) *He experienced God's Compassion*

God loves us so much that He seldom leaves us without the help of reliable human companionship. This is one of the practical ways in which He demonstrates His love for us. In the midst of this extremely dangerous situation Jonathan took the risk of going to the Wilderness of Ziph to meet his friend solely in order to strengthen his hand in God (23:16). Saul's spies were everywhere and we have already seen that the men of this area were not kindly disposed towards David. Jonathan met him and said: "Fear not: for the hand of Saul my father shall not find thee; and thou shalt be king over Israel, and I shall be next unto thee . . . And they two made a covenant before the Lord" (23:17-18). In time of need good friends are one of life's choicest blessings. Jonathan's qualities continue to impress the Christian as he reads these chapters. He was not lacking in *courage* and made the journey to Ziph even though he knew that his father's soldiers were searching that area every day (23:14). It was all the more risky in that the king did not only want to know David's whereabouts but he was eager to discover who was meeting David (23:22), so it was a highly dangerous mission. Jonathan knew full well what it might cost him if he had been found by Saul's troops in that region.

Jonathan's *encouragement* also meant much to David at this time. His words to the fugitive exactly matched his need. David was certainly frightened (cf. 23:15 RSV) and he may well have been wondering about God's purpose for the future. What was the meaning of life if a man had to spend his time hiding in caves and dens? But the young prince reassured him as he quietly said: "Fear not . . . thou shalt be king over Israel."

Again David must have been overwhelmed by his friend's utter *humility*. Jonathan said: "I shall be next unto thee."

He was such a self-effacing man and never looked upon David as a rival for the crown, for he was only anxious to be in God's will himself. He had a deep spiritual awareness that God wanted David on the throne and so he was quite content with a subordinate place: "I shall be next unto thee." The words brought great comfort to David though they expressed an ambition that was never realized.

Just at a time when he felt deeply depressed and fearful, God sent Jonathan to David's side. There was no time for a long conversation, but in only a few minutes Jonathan brought immense peace to David's troubled spirit. He had just the right word to say. One of the things which distressed Job in his trouble was that his friends did not bring him the help he needed. They acknowledged that his words had "set men on their feet" (Job 4:4 Moffatt's translation) but their own words caused Job to suffer even greater agony. In this anguish he cried out "how forcible are right words!" (Job 6:25). The Book of Proverbs emphasizes the importance of having the right thing to say to people in need: "A word fitly spoken is like apples of gold in pictures of silver" (Prov. 25:11). Jonathan was a man who uplifted his friend by what he had to say. He was God's choice gift to David in that time of bleak despair. Christian people should always pray that they will be equally faithful to their friends in trouble.

### (c) *He trusted God's Wisdom*

There is something else of importance in this story. When we are in trouble we must believe that God will intervene at the right moment in a time of crisis. David was overwhelmed by his troubles and Saul's troops were closing in on him. Within a few hours they would certainly have captured him when, suddenly, a messenger arrived to tell Saul that the Philistines were making a series of devastating raids on his territories and he had to abandon his pursuit of David. In any kind of adversity we too need to remember that God is sovereign and He will not forsake us. Saul could control the movements of his own soldiers in the Wilderness of Ziph but he could do nothing about the plans of the Philistines. Without doubt, the Philistine diversion was the direct intervention of a sovereign and omnipotent God. We may sometimes be tempted to think that our problems are insuperable but God is able to meet us in our extremity and give us all the help we need. The apostle Paul underlined this truth to the church at Corinth and assured them that in all troubles and temptations God provides a "way of escape" (1 Cor. 10:13 RSV). David hoped and prayed that Saul would give up his search but there was nothing he could do about it. At a time when His servant's life was in danger, God drew Saul's soldiers away from the scene.

### (d) He manifested God's Mercy

One final thing emerges in this story. It concerns David's refusal to harbour any bitterness or resentment. Once Saul had vanquished the Philistines, he returned to his fanatical pursuit and once again David's life was in danger. The king's informers assured him that his enemy was hiding somewhere in the Wilderness of Engedi, so Saul resumed his search in that area. One day he entered and slept in the very cave where David and his men were sheltering. David could easily have killed the king and his men urged him to do so, but he refused. He was obviously aware of the low spiritual and moral state of the nation. After the massacre of innocent people at Nob many could have argued that it was better to shed Saul's blood than allow him to live and continue to murder hundreds more. But David could not argue in that way. He had a deep sense of respect and awe. Saul was "the Lord's anointed" (24:6) and if only Saul would leave him in peace, David was eager to save him. He clearly referred to him as "my lord" (24:6 RSV). A piece of cloth was cut from Saul's robe as he slept to prove to the king that it had been in David's power to assassinate him. David still hoped for peace and reconciliation and pleaded with Saul to bring the bitterness to an end (24:9-15). He had refused to act as Saul's judge when he was in the cave. His prayer in the cave is found in the Book of Psalms (Ps. 57) and David there affirmed that God fulfils His purpose for His children (Ps. 57:2). He proved God's faithfulness: "He shall send from heaven, and save me" (Ps. 57:3). God had done just that and had used some Philistine raiders to execute His will. In that psalm David also gave expression to his conviction that it is God who puts to shame those who trample upon us (Ps. 57:3 RSV). Far from taking vengeance into his own hands he begged the king to put away his hatred, and left it for Saul to make the next move. The king seemed to be deeply sorry at the time and returned to his palace. But his anger was to return and the feud was not over although David had done his utmost to heal the breach. When there is any kind of trouble in relationships Christians must follow David's rich example. Any kind of bitterness has to be confessed and forsaken. For David to have shared Saul's anger would have robbed him of that spiritual strength and serenity which saw him through many a difficult day. In the cave he had cast himself upon God's mercy: "Be merciful unto me, O God" (Ps. 57:1). For this reason he could not think of taking Saul's life. A man cannot cry "Be merciful unto me, O God" and then be merciless to one of God's children, no matter how rebellious or difficult that man may be. Many centuries later the Lord Jesus made a plea to His disciples: "Love ye your enemies, and do good . . . Be ye therefore merciful, as your Father also is merciful" (Luke 6:35-36).

# 8

# THREE PEOPLE IN TROUBLE

People react to trouble in a variety of ways. Some folk go to pieces; others seem to grow in spiritual stature and take great forward strides in courageous confidence. Some reveal qualities that few would have realized they possessed, while others show signs of hidden weakness and insecure faith. In the next section of the narrative (1 Samuel chapters 25 to 30) we see three people's reactions to serious difficulties in their lives. They have obvious lessons for us.

I AVOID BITTERNESS—*When in trouble remember Abigail* The wonderful thing about Abigail is that when she meets trouble she is used to bring good out of it. A careful reading of 1 Samuel 25 shows us that during his highly precarious and unsettled existence David and his men acted as unofficial protectors of a wealthy farmer's sheep (25:15-16). This man, Nabal, had never invited them to do this work for him but in view of frequent raids by Philistine brigands (23:27) it had obviously been to his advantage that David's men had patrolled the entire area and warded off any suspecting thieves. Nabal's shepherds freely confessed their indebtedness to the fugitives and described them as "a wall unto us both by night and day" (25:16). David's men had provided this service without reward of any kind but now they were desperately hungry and in great material need, so David asked Nabal if he could supply some food for his companions. He chose the right moment to make the request. Sheep-shearing was over and it was a feast day (25:2, 8). Such times were occasions for merriment and generosity (cf. 2.Sam. 13:23-24). At such a moment a wealthy

74

landowner could afford to be kind to the needy, but Nabal was well known in the locality for a sullen manner and an extremely mean disposition. He refused to give bread to David's men and, quite naturally, this aroused David's anger. He knew that his men completely outnumbered Nabal's shepherds. In a fit of temper, David gathered most of his men together, intent on killing Nabal and his household (25:22) but Nabal's wife, Abigail, intervened. It is a magnificent story of quiet heroism and peace-loving compassion and stands in Holy Scripture in contrast and rebuke to David's hastiness and impetuous action. Loading a generous supply of food and wine on to her servants' asses she went out to meet David. She took her life into her hands and, on meeting him, freely confessed her husband's error. She told David that her husband was true to his name; it meant "fool". As Abigail interceded she explained that Nabal had acted with typical lack of wisdom but went on to talk about David rather than about him; her plea is a model of wise and judicious speech in a most critical situation. She appealed to David to avoid taking vengeance for by so doing he would be guilty of Saul's sin. Entirely innocent people could easily have been slain in a moment of anger and the sin would be no less serious and offensive to God than the massacre at Nob. David had been terribly shocked by Saul's heartless atrocity there only a few weeks before, but now he was about to do the same himself. It is strange how fiercely we speak about the sins of others whilst we can easily tolerate our own (cf. Matt. 7:1-5).

Abigail was willing to be an intercessor (25:23-24). Obviously she was not personally responsible for her husband's sin but she took its shame upon herself in sincere penitence and confession. Many of God's servants in Old Testament times were so deeply sensitive that when they came to confess the nation's sin they clearly identified themselves with the offenders. Ezra (9:1–10:1), Nehemiah (1:5-7) and Daniel (9:3-23) are three outstanding examples of this kind of spiritual sensitivity.

At that time there were very few in Israel who were prepared to speculate about the eventual outcome of the tension between Saul and David. It had to end some time but Jonathan was one of the few who believed that David would ultimately be king (23:17). Samuel had obviously believed that David would reign one day but now he was dead (25:1). What an encouragement it must have been for David to hear Abigail's confident words so soon after those of Jonathan (25:28-30). She really believed in David and his cause. She did not exalt him personally, but she did speak openly about what the Lord was doing for him and through him. She used a phrase which must have rejoiced David's heart for it recalled his encounter with Goliath. Abigail referred to the fact that he was fighting "the battles of the Lord" (25:28, cf. 17:47). Her words about the Lord slinging David's enemies "as out of the middle of a sling" (25:29) may be an intentional attempt to remind David of the Goliath encounter. The sling had played an important part in that battle (17:40) and perhaps Abigail was saying in effect: "You cannot use a stone and sling against your present giant (Saul) and his armies, but God will hurl them out of your way if you will trust and honour Him."

Abigail begged David not to take vengeance into his own hands for she believed that the matter should be left in the just and righteous hands of God Himself, not man (25:30-31, 37-39). She simply reminded him of God's law about this (Lev. 19:18). It was a truth which had to be impressed on David at that particular moment. He had to realize that vengeance was God's concern and not his. Only a few weeks later, David walked through Saul's encampment at the dead of night (26:5-12) and stood with his friend, Abishai, looking into the face of Saul as he slept. Abishai invited David to put an end to all this anguish by killing Saul and, at that precise moment, David probably remembered the incident of Nabal and the wise words of Abigail. Confronted with the opportunity of taking vengeance into his own hands he whispered to Abishai: "Destroy him not . . . the Lord shall smite him . . .

The Lord forbid that I should stretch forth mine hand against the Lord's anointed" (26:9-11). When we are sinned against we are sometimes tempted to take matters into our own hands and in some subtle way try to "get our own back", but we must remember Paul's words to his Christian friends in Rome: "Beloved, never avenge yourselves, but leave it to the wrath of God" (Rom. 12:19 RSV). Many of Paul's readers were to be cruelly sinned against by their pagan neighbours but before the bitter persecution came he reminded them of this divine instruction (cf. Lev. 19:18; Deut. 32:35).

2 AVOID UNGUIDED ACTIONS—*When in trouble remember David*

We turn now to 1 Samuel chapters 26-27 and 29-30. These narratives tell us quite plainly that we must take care not to rely merely on our own wisdom when we are in difficulties. Once again David had spared Saul's life (26:1-25) but he was obviously afraid of the king and, utterly frustrated by Saul's continuing persecution, and suffering because of the obvious deprivation, David gathered his men and sought refuge in Philistine territory, making for Gath, a well-fortified Philistine city. Although he had earlier made a special point of discerning God's mind (23:2), David simply went off to live with the Philistines without seeking guidance at all. It was an unfortunate compromise and a terrible mistake. His anxiety is understandable. He realized by now that he could not possibly hope for any kind of reconciliation with Saul. He knew he was being pursued by a mentally sick tyrant and there was little hope of peace. It was natural for David to be emotionally disturbed and physically weary but, for some reason or other, he had become spiritually insensitive. Achish, the King of Gath, was happy to have David. He knew of his valiant exploits in the past and it was better to have David's courageous men on his side rather than against him. But David was foolish to go to Gath without the assurance that this was God's will for him at this particular

77

time. His hasty, unguided decision only led him into further trouble. This kind of thing can happen to us. When we are in difficulty it is natural to consider what is the best thing to do; more than anything else we want to get away from our trouble. That is *not necessarily* God's will for us. He wants us to get *above it* not away from it. On another occasion David wished he had the wings of a dove to fly away from his distress (Ps. 55:6) but the prophet Isaiah said that God prefers to give us the wings of an eagle (Isa. 40:31) to soar high above our troubles and so be enabled to look down on them and see them as God sees them. If we are in distress we ought to seek Him all the more. We go quickly to our friends for advice but we should hurry into God's presence in an endeavour to understand exactly what He wants us to do.

For a while everything seemed to go all right for David. He told King Achish that he was raiding the towns of Judah whereas in reality he was attacking Judah's enemies (27: 8-12). He was working for his own country even though he no longer lived in it, but he could not hope to keep up this ridiculous act for long. The lie was bound to be discovered. True, David was safe from Saul (27:4) but he had merely run from one enemy to another. Inevitably the day came when Achish planned a major encounter with Saul's armies (28: 1-2), a real one and not a make-believe attack like David's. He naturally expected that the fugitive who had led so many successful minor skirmishes would play a leading part in a large-scale offensive. David's silly scheme was all over. The Philistine soldiers were soon assembled together with David's men among them (29:1-2). It must have been an awful moment for David—to think that he would soon meet his own kinsmen face to face and be expected to slay them in battle. Decisions which are made without guidance can often lead to more serious difficulty. Mercifully, the Lord God intervened by sowing suspicion in the minds of some of Achish's senior officers. As the troops were being inspected (29:3-5) these Philistine commanders insisted that

David's men be sent back in case they went over to the side of their own countrymen at a crucial moment in the battle. God had delivered David in this way. He was told to return to Gath with his men. On their journey they found that a troop of Amalekite brigands had raided the Judaean town of Ziklag (30:1-5). They had set fire to the city and taken away the women and children. Some of these families belonged to David's men and David shared their anguish and loss but, for the first time, his own men turned against him. Fearing that their wives and children had been slain they talked about taking David's life in vengeance (30:6). In his distress. David asked for God's guidance (30:7-8). What a pity he had not done this earlier before he went over to the Philistines. As we have seen, when we rely on our own ideas, we often multiply our troubles rather than remove them. God came to David's aid and the women and children of Ziklag were saved (30:9-19).

3 AVOID DISOBEDIENCE—*When in trouble remember Saul*
For this sad story, we turn to 1 Samuel chapter 28. We have just seen that when in trouble David was led into greater distress by failing to seek the mind of God. Saul, on the other hand, did try to discover God's will when the armies of Achish came out against him, but it was too late. Guidance can not be turned on and off like a tap. The king of Israel had persistently refused to listen to the warning voice of God and had killed a number of priests whose task it was to discern the divine will. He made the mistake, of which we may also be guilty at times, of ignoring the Lord until he really wanted something he could obtain in no other way. In his rebellion and disobedience God had nothing to say to him. Maintaining constant communion with the Lord is as important in days of prosperity as in times of crisis. Always keep the lines of communication open. If we persistently refuse to heed God's Word the time may come when, suffering from some kind of spiritual atrophy, we shall not be able to hear Him.

Terrified at the prospect of military defeat and national collapse, Saul tried to listen for the quiet reassuring word of God but it never came (28:6). His own loud voice over the years had repeatedly drowned the pleading whisper of God in his own soul. Now there was nothing but a frightening and foreboding silence. When God would not speak, Saul thought about resorting to witchcraft, although he had "put the mediums and the wizards out of the land" (28:3,9 RSV). What a dreadful hypocrite he was. Like many other people over the centuries, he demanded high standards from others but lived quite contentedly with lower ones for himself (cf. Matt. 23:2-4; S. of S. 1:6).

Witchcraft was expressly forbidden by the Mosaic Law (Lev. 19:31, Deut. 18:10-12). How could Saul hope to be comforted when he was seeking a message by a means which God had definitely prohibited? He left the scene of his unlawful inquiry a broken and shattered man, realizing that his cause was completely lost. Years before he had threatened to kill any medium or witch he discovered in the land (28:9). Now he was made to hear his own death sentence in the presence of such an evil person (28:19). In our trouble we may be exposed to all kinds of sinister temptations. In agonizing bereavement and deep distress, even deeply committed Christians have been tempted to attend a spiritualist meeting in the hope of receiving some message from a loved one. Spiritism is forbidden; it is devilish and doomed. It cannot possibly help us. This narrative makes it clear that Samuel did not want to be disturbed by the living when he had entered the realm of the dead. When we are anxious and grieved, the Devil may well tempt us to get relief from any source whatever, as long as we are comforted. But to disobey God's Word is to close the door to any possibility of divine help when we most need it. Those who refuse to obey His voice cannot hope to receive His peace.

# 9

# SEVEN UNHAPPY YEARS

In this chapter we shall study the closing scene in the life of
Saul and the opening events in the reign of David (1 Sam.
31–2 Sam. 4). The tragic death of both Saul and Jonathan
marks the transition from the First to the Second book of
Samuel. Some outstanding qualities shine out as bright lights
over a dark and depressing landscape.

## (a) *The loyalty of an armour bearer*

He did not forget *Saul's dignity*. The king was seriously
wounded. He knew that Jonathan had been slain and, obviously aware of his utter defeat, Saul longed to die. He begged
his armour bearer to kill him, but the man knew that the
king had once been publicly anointed as God's servant and
refused to do so. Contrast the faithfulness and devotion
of this loyal armour bearer with the Amalekite liar who
tried to win David's favour with his fanciful story about
Saul's death (2 Sam. 1:2ff., cf. 2 Sam. 4:10). We should note
incidentally, that the account of Saul's death (1 Sam.
31:4ff.) is one of the very rare cases of suicide in the Old
Testament.

## (b) *The courage of the men of Jabesh*

They did not forget *Saul's kindness* (1 Sam. 31:8-13). Many
years before, Saul had saved their lives (1 Sam. 11:12f.) and,
though in the intervening years he had disappointed the
people, the men of Jabesh did not forget all that he had done
for them in the hour of their great need. In an extremely
dangerous mission, they recovered Saul's body from its place
of shame and buried it in their own city. The men of Jabesh

knew only too well of Saul's failures but preferred to think of his kindness to them. We can easily become so obsessed with people's faults that we entirely forget the many good things about them.

### (c) *The devotion of David*

He did not forget *Saul's valour*. The Second Book of Samuel opens with this beautiful elegy, sometimes called "The Song of the Bow" (2 Sam. 1:17-27). It is not only one of the finest passages in literature but a striking tribute to David as a man. As king, Saul had been a pathetic failure but David refused to overlook his achievements. He deliberately recalled some good things about him. He remembered Saul's physical beauty (19), unrivalled strength (21, "the shield of the mighty"), royal dignity (21, "anointed with oil"), military success (22), personal attractiveness (23) and unsparing generosity (24). David grieved that Israel had lost its king and that he had lost his closest friend, Jonathan.

After the death of Saul there was a tragic period of national disunity during which part of the country was ruled by Ishbosheth, Saul's son, and part by David. The first seven and a half years of David's rule was centred on the city of Hebron (5:4-5) and these years brought him even more grief than his five as a fugitive in exile. We must notice three factors about this period:

(a) The new reign began in the *spirit of deep reliance upon God for guidance*. David had obviously learned a good deal from his earlier mistakes (1 Sam. 27:1-3) so he now asked God for clear direction about his future (2 Sam. 2:1). He wanted to be quite sure that he was doing the right thing, and we see this illustrated again in a later narrative (5:19). Seeking God's guidance is of the utmost importance in the life of every believer. We often make the mistake of imagining that guidance is something we seek for the really big decisions of life, but we are not likely to discern God's will for what we imagine to be important things if we do not ask

Him to guide us in ordinary everyday affairs. The new king did not merely seek God's will; he sought to be obedient to it: "And David did so, as the Lord had commanded him" (5:25).

(b) Further, the new reign began with a determination to *remember the kindness and generosity of others*. Once David had made Hebron his base he had a multitude of things to attend to, but his first task was to send for the men of Jabesh-gilead to talk with them and reward them for their courageous action in recovering Saul's body. He wanted to acknowledge their faithfulness. It may also have crossed David's mind to meet these valiant men in the hope that the loyalty they had shown to Saul would be transferred to him, but whatever his motives he expressed his gratitude to the men of Jabesh for their kindness to Saul. David might well have argued that he had enough to get on with trying to establish the kingdom without spending his time commending a group of valiant citizens, but he refused to ignore the good deeds of others; they were worthy of his special interest and personal commendation. The Lord clearly expects us to take keen interest in other people's Christian work and not to become totally immersed in our own little corner. It is so easy to become preoccupied with what is happening in our own church and to forget the work and witness of neighbouring churches, or to be so keen on what is happening in our own locality that we ignore the needs of the mission field.

(c) One thing more: the new reign began with a series of tragic events reminding the new king of the *heartbreaking effect of sin*. Each one of the five chapters before us records at least one tragic death. During these years, whilst the leadership of the nation was divided between David and Ishbosheth, there was constant friction between David's soldiers (led by Joab) and Ishbosheth's men (under the authority of Abner). These two military captains are a study in themselves. Abner was obviously the power behind Ishbosheth, and Joab had far more influence and responsibility than was good for him or for David. It is a tragic story and a further grim illustration of the power of sin to reproduce itself. If we reconstruct the scene it is apparent that there must have been bitterness in the hearts of the soldiers at Gibeon to turn a friendly display into an unexpected massacre. This horrible encounter led to the serious battle in which Abner was defeated. Asahel pursued Abner in the hope of killing him but was killed himself. This created deeper bitterness in the heart of Joab and eventually led to Abner's death. The deeply committed Christian knows that sin must not be allowed to become reproduced in his life in this way, and prays that it may die within him. Dr. G. B. Caird has put it this way: "Evil propagates itself by a chain reaction. It is like a bad coin which is passed on from one person to another until it reaches someone who will put it out of currency by absorbing the loss ... Evil is defeated only if the injured person absorbs the evil and refuses to allow it to go any further." (*Principalities and Powers*)

In these passages, we take note of David's *impossible attempt to free himself from blame.* When he heard of Abner's murder by Joab, he cried out "I and my kingdom are guiltless ..." (3:28). But it was not nearly so simple. David has *some* responsibility for this vicious act. He was partly to blame for having such an unscrupulous man at the head of his army. In many ways he had asked for the trouble he got both then and later. He could no more escape the guilt than Pilate could centuries later (Matt. 27:24). We all love to plunge our sin-stained hands into a basin and loudly protest our innocence, but it is rarely possible to do so in deep sincerity. We all carry some kind of responsibility for the sin of others. More virile witness for Christ, higher moral standards, keener spiritual ambitions, a more friendly spirit, all would make for a better community in which sinning would not be so easy. When the people of the French town of Ars were asked to explain the complete change of moral life in their community, they pointed to the famous Curé and said "There are some things you cannot do when there's a saint about." Our lack of holiness may well be the almost imperceptible beginning of somebody else's downfall.

# 10

# THE KING COMES TO JERUSALEM

2 Samuel 5-6 records a series of important events which mark the beginning of David's reign over the entire land. The narrative can be divided into five scenes.

1 A NEW ALLEGIANCE TO STRENGTHEN THE KING (2 Sam. 5:1-5)
After the death of Ishbosheth the previously disunited tribes united to confess their allegiance to David. In doing so they mentioned three things about him which they found attractive:

(*a*) *Natural affinity*
   When they met him they knew they were in the presence of one who had the same things at heart as themselves. "Behold, we are thy bone and thy flesh" (5:1).

(*b*) *Personal ability*
   They knew David to be a born leader; even as a homeless fugitive, he had helped the people of his own nation in their difficulties and distress (5:2).

(*c*) *Spiritual Authority*
   The people recognized that God had chosen him to be their new king: "*and the Lord said to thee*, Thou shalt feed my people Israel, and thou shalt be a captain over Israel" (5:2).
   All those Israelites who came before David that day, assuring him of their loyalty, had discerned a divinely

ordained authority in all his actions. If God calls a man, He equips him. The Lord had clearly said to the young shepherd of Bethlehem that He had a far bigger flock for him to lead and protect: "You shall be shepherd of my people Israel" (2 Sam. 5:2 RSV).

## 2 AN OUTSTANDING VICTORY TO ESTABLISH THE KING (2 Sam. 5:6-25)

Once the nation was united under David's leadership two great military exploits followed in quick succession. We note, first of all, *an internal problem* (5:6ff.). The Jebusites refused to acknowledge David's sovereignty but David knew that the strategic city of Jerusalem must be conquered and used as a capital; it had so many advantages. But its arrogant citizens stubbornly rejected his leadership. In over-confident taunts they said that the city was so well fortified that even its blind and crippled citizens could ward off an attack (5:6). It was perfectly true, of course, that the city had massive fortifications. It was probably over a thousand years old at that time so had withstood the ravages and onslaughts of many centuries, but the city was captured. Josephus, the famous historian, says that David's soldiers entered the impregnable fortress of Jerusalem by way of a watershaft (5:8 RSV).

The new king now had his magnificent capital but he soon needed to employ all his military strategy again. The internal problem was quickly followed by *an external difficulty* (5:17-25). Hearing that David had been crowned as king over a united Israel, the Philistine armies came marching into his newly-occupied territories. David earnestly sought the guidance of God (5:19) and his reliance was rewarded by a glorious victory. The battle was such an outstanding example of God's power to rout Israel's enemies that the place was thereafter called Baal-perazim which meant "Lord of breaking-through" (RSV). If we in our turn seek God's mind and purpose for every step of our lives and rely utterly upon Him, He will lead us and *break through* all opposing forces in our lives. David's desire to honour God is further illustrated by his destruction of the Philistine idols left on the battlefield. He knew how powerless those gods were, so burned them all.

Whilst we are considering this encounter we should note that, although David had been made aware of God's clear direction before he attacked the Philistines, he did not make the mistake of presuming that the particular orders given in this instance were to be applied for all times. When the Philistines sent more troops into his land, the heathen armies were arrayed at exactly the same place as the first battalions which had been overwhelmingly defeated. It would have been natural to act on the basis of an earlier revelation and do exactly the same as before but David knew that God might have entirely different plans this time—and He did. The first time God told him to meet the army by direct attack (5:19-20). On the second occasion he was told to go behind and ambush them. It was a test of faith. The king was naturally eager to subdue his enemies but was told that he must quietly wait until he heard the wind rustling the leaves of the mulberry trees. In the stillness it would seem like the sound of marching feet. At that precise moment David could be assured that God's unseen host was fighting alongside the king's soldiers. It was a moment of resounding victory and, at the end of the day, David once again returned home a conqueror. The story of the two Philistine attacks illustrates an important spiritual principle. Sometimes God immediately gives us clear and unmistakable guidance. At other times, as in the second story (5:22-25), we are given the next step and then instructed to wait for further orders. At such times we may become impatient and even irritated by the delay but do well to remind ourselves that "It is good that a man should both hope and quietly wait for the salvation of the Lord" (Lam. 3:26).

The Bible is utterly true to life. How often we experience some great victory or spiritual achievement in our lives and then, as we are rejoicing and exulting in all its thrill and wonder, suddenly become guilty of some stupid sin, careless deed or disobedient action. The king longed to establish the newly captured city of Jerusalem as a spiritual centre of worship and it was natural that he should want to bring the ark of the covenant into the city, but his enthusiasm got the better of his wisdom. The ark had been constructed so that it could be carried by means of two poles. Furthermore, God had planned that its transportation should always be undertaken by priests (Deut. 10:8; 31:9); this was part of God's law and should have been fully obeyed. Yet David allowed the people to put the ark on to a cart drawn by oxen. On the journey a man named Uzzah reached forward to steady the ark and, on doing so, collapsed and died. If David had remembered God's Word the accident would not have happened and he quickly realized his mistake. Later he says to the priests. "Ye are the chief of the fathers of the Levites: sanctify yourselves . . . that ye may bring up the ark of the Lord God of Israel unto the place that I have prepared for it. For because ye did it not at the first, the Lord our God made a breach upon us, for that *we sought him not after the due order*" (1 Chron. 15:12f.).

David's desire to bring the ark into the city was a perfectly good one but he ought to have made sure he was doing it in the way that pleased God. A church officer might well have the best interests of his church at heart and may genuinely long for its highest good but yet in his service be self-important and resentful of any suggestion as to how his work can be improved. Nobody can find fault with what he does for God but it is the way he does it that is so offensive. This was David's mistake. God is not only interested in motives; He is also concerned about methods.

## 4 A GREAT FESTIVAL TO ENCOURAGE THE KING (2 Sam. 6:11-19)

Aware of God's apparent disfavour, the king would not permit his servants to continue their dangerous journey, so the ark was taken into the house of Obed-Edom ("servant of Edom"), a Gentile who lived near the scene of the accident. All the time the ark was in his home, the household was richly blessed. It is possible that the tragic death of Uzzah and the events which followed led to the conversion of this family for we know that, later on, Obed-Edom joined the Israelite procession of thanksgiving. It is unlikely that he would have been allowed to do this if he had still retained his allegiance to the Edomite gods (1 Chron. 15:21). Later still, he went into the service of the ark in the Sanctuary (1 Chron. 15:24; 16:4-5). Tragedies can often be used by God to lead to great spiritual triumphs. When God reigns all is not lost for He can bring good out of any disaster.

The king knew at this point that it was safe to continue the ark's journey and the psalm he sang as it entered Jerusalem expounds some great spiritual themes (1 Chron. 16:7-36; cf. Ps. 96:1-13; Ps. 105:1-15). The more important ones can be summarized in this way:

Rejoice – Give thanks for the *present* (1 Chron. 16:8-10)
Rely – Trust Him for the *future* (1 Chron. 16:11)
Remember – Remember His goodness in the *past* (1 Chron 16:12, 15-22)

## 5 AN OLD PROBLEM TO TROUBLE THE KING (2 Sam. 6:20-23)

David was overjoyed that the ark was to be safely installed in the sanctuary in Jerusalem and in his exuberant gaiety he danced at the head of the procession. Everyone in Jerusalem shared his joyful enthusiasm, except Michal, who looked out from her window and despised her husband. All the men of Israel returned home to bless their households and David also returned home in that same spirit of gratitude and joy. But the king was met by an unspiritual wife who sneered at him for laying aside his royal garments and dancing in the streets of Jerusalem just like any other man. Michal hated this. She was proud and arrogant and would not humble herself before God. In the streets the king had been surrounded by equally grateful citizens but in his own house he was greeted with sarcasm and bitterness. How grateful many of us should be for a happy and spiritually united home life. David's marriage to Michal was an appalling mistake. It is far better to stay single than to marry an unbeliever. No Christian can hope to prosper if he or she deliberately ignores God's Word about this important matter. Those sad moments at the close of David's happy day are recorded in Scripture as a warning to all.

# II

# HOME AND FOREIGN AFFAIRS

Once the ark was safely installed in its sanctuary-tent in Jerusalem, the king set his mind to the ordering of several national issues and, in the next main section of the narrative, we read of a number of his ventures in home and foreign affairs (2 Sam. 7-10). It can be divided into four sections.

1 DAVID'S AMBITION (2 Sam. 7:1-11a)
In accordance with the Law of Moses the ark had been carefully placed in a special tent, but the king became disturbed because it did not seem right that he should live in a magnificent palace whilst the ark was in a temporary dwelling place. A tent was the lodging of a nomad, the lowest and least significant member in the social structure of the Hebrew people. Surely, thought David, the ark was worthy of a permanent building. It seemed to him that he was offering God far less than he had himself and David wanted to give God the best. In this he was setting a high standard to the nation. It is a sad thing that the people did not keep David's sense of spiritual priorities. Most of the later kings preferred to please themselves rather than honour God. Some of the outstanding prophets of the Old Testament took great risks in later centuries by exposing the nation's sin of putting self interests first and giving priorities to their own comforts, often to the utter exclusion of God's work and the crying needs of some of His people (Amos 6:4-6; Haggai 1:4, Mal. 1:8, 13). Sometimes God has far less than our best but over the centuries the saints have preferred to put God first and give Him their all. C. T. Studd, the outstanding mission-

ary, expressed it in famous words: "If Jesus Christ be God and died for me then no sacrifice can be too great for me to make for Him."

David, therefore, determined to provide a permanent home for the ark, and talked it over with a faithful court-prophet, Nathan (7:2). Naturally, Nathan was delighted at the thought of seeing a proper building for spiritual worship. It would give outward expression to the gratitude and dependence of thousands of devout Israelites. But that night God told Nathan that the work of building the Temple was to be the responsibility of David's son, Solomon. Nathan knew that David had set his heart (7:3) on building the Temple but he had the courage to share with the king the truths which God had revealed to him. Nathan was given an even more difficult message to deliver some years later (2 Sam. 12:1-15). His faithfulness in boldly proclaiming God's Word ought to be a constant rebuke to our self-protective cowardice and fear.

## 2 DAVID'S HOUSE (2 Sam. 7:11b-29)

In the message which God gave Nathan for David there is a play on words which can be easily missed. David had expressed a deep desire to build a "house" for God (7:1-2) but God told him that He would build a "house" for David (7:11b). Notice how God repeated His promise to the king (7:16) almost as if to emphasize how much He valued David's spiritual priorities. By "David's house" God obviously meant that the royal line would be kept in his family and it was a lovely thing for God to show His love for David in this way. In the Chronicler's account of this incident we are told why David was not permitted to build the Temple; it was not thought fitting that a man who had been involved in so many wars should build God's house. The task was to be left to Solomon, and there is probably another subtle word-play here, for his name comes from the same root as *shalom* meaning "peace".

Before we leave this account it is encouraging to note that

although the king was not allowed to build the Temple, the Lord God was pleased that the idea was in his heart. Solomon later remembered this truth and mentioned in his prayer of dedication that God had told his father: "thou didst well that it was in thine heart" (1 Kgs. 8:18). We cannot always realize all our spiritual dreams or fulfil all our lofty ambitions. A young man wants to go to the mission field but ill-health makes it impossible. A young woman eagerly looks forward to a nursing career but unexpected home responsibilities make it difficult. God knows all about it and says, as He did to David, "thou didst well that it was in thine heart".

3 DAVID'S EMPIRE (2 Sam. 8:1-18)
Chapter 8 records David's unhindered victories and outstanding military exploits and more than once it is said that the king was protected by God. David's success was not merely due to his ability as a valiant soldier. "The Lord gave victory to David" (8:6, 14 RSV). The king did not take this divine protection for granted but expressed his gratitude by dedicating everything to God (8:11). We have already seen that David put God first (7:1-29). The man who does this will never lack God's provision. Centuries later Jesus assured His disciples of this same truth: "If any man serve Me, him will my Father honour" (John 12:26; cf. Mark 10:29-30; Matt. 6:33). David marched to a hundred different victories because God was on his side.

4 DAVID'S GENEROSITY (2 Sam. 9:1–10:19)
David can be seen here as a human personality with an immense capacity for love. The two stories are set side by side as if to illustrate his abundant generosity and uninhibited love. In the one case this generosity was eagerly accepted and in the other it was ungraciously spurned.

(a) Kindness in home affairs (9:1-13)
This is a moving illustration of David's genuine com-

passion and deep concern for Jonathan's heir. Mephibosheth. Years before he had made his close friend a solemn promise that he would be kind to all his household (1 Sam. 20:14-17, 42) and now David had the opportunity of giving practical expression to that sacred vow. He inquired as to the whereabouts of Mephibosheth and was told that the crippled lad was in Lo-debar ("the place of no pasture"); it must have touched David's heart. He knew full well the meaning of the name and it must have recalled his early days as a shepherd on the hills of Bethlehem. Every good shepherd loved his sheep and could not bear to leave them without pasture (cf. Ps. 23:2). This story is a magnificent parable of our redemption. We too have been taken crippled and helpless from our own "Lo-debar" and brought by our Good Shepherd to a place of rich provision and eternal safety (John 10:9,11, 27-29).

(b) *Kindness in foreign affairs* (10:19)
The second story tells of David's kindness to a newly-crowned monarch, Hanun, King of Ammon. Hanun's father had been good to David in former years and David wanted to pay his respects to the new king. Hanun was young, and carelessly taking the advice of some of his statesmen, he publicly humiliated David's ambassadors and sent them back to their home country. It was a foolish thing to do and led to warfare and bloodshed. Just as the previous story can be seen as a parable of God's grace, so this story can be interpreted as a parable of man's stubborn refusal to receive God's free and generous love. God has sent many of His messengers into this world with a word of peace, love and reconciliation but they have been cruelly treated (Matt. 23:34-37). Finally, He sent His Son (Mark 12:6-8) to plead with men to be reconciled and at peace with God (Eph. 2:17; 2 Cor. 5:18-19) but even He was despised and rejected by men (Isa. 53:3). Hanun and the Ammonites were punished for their suspicion, cruelty and stubborn rejection of peace (2 Sam. 11:1) and man's persistent refusal to hear God's

pleading word of forgiveness and peace will inevitably bring its own serious judgment (John 3:36).

God's love for us can either be gratefully accepted (as Mephibosheth) or ungraciously spurned (as Hanun). Those who turn away from His love bring anguish and hurt upon themselves whilst those who accept His mercy enjoy His favour and receive His gifts. These stories from David's life expound the seriousness and simplicity of the gospel.

# 12

# BLOT OUT MY TRANSGRESSIONS

We come now to what is surely the most distressing episode in David's life. We have seen earlier that the Bible is completely honest in its account of the exploits and activities of its leading characters. No attempt is made to minimize the seriousness of their sins, whether it is Noah's drunkenness (Gen. 9:20-21), Abraham's lying (Gen. 12:11-20; 20:1-18), Moses' hasty temper (Exod. 2:12, Num. 20:10ff.), Gideon's greed (Judg. 8:24-27), David's adultery (2 Sam. 11:1-5) or Jeremiah's resentment (Jer. 15:18). The biblical narratives are completely truthful. Despite the fact that David became a national hero, the Holy Spirit does not allow us to have a one-sided picture of his life. He was a man like us, a man who could manifest great love and kindness (9:1-13) and yet be utterly heartless and cruel (11:1-27).

The tragic story of David's sin is told in 2 Samuel chapters 11 and 12, and we shall take a careful look at the five characters in this pathetic drama. They provide us with yet another grim illustration of the way in which sin reproduces itself. There is hardly any such thing as a secret sin. By its very nature sin quickly begets other sins and seriously affects the lives of other people. Once it is set on its course it is hard to stop its terrifying reproductive process. David's sin obviously affected Bathsheba, but it rapidly struck at her innocent husband, Uriah. Before long, another army officer, Joab, was seriously involved and, in the end, it brought grief to the heart of the sensitive prophet Nathan.

I DAVID—THE MAIN OFFENDER
This tragic sequence of events had its sad beginning in idle-

ness and inactivity. The chapter which records the awful story (2 Sam. 11) starts by telling us that other kings had gone forth to war but David stayed at home, content to send a deputy to the battlefield. If David had marched out of Jerusalem at the head of his army the Bathsheba incident might never have happened. Idleness exposes any Christian to a multitude of subtle and serious temptations. Martin Luther used to illustrate it in graphic terms: ". . . the human heart, unless it be occupied with some employment, leaves space for the devil, who wriggles himself in and brings with him a whole host of evil thoughts, temptations and tribulations".

Observe the downward steps of the sinner. "David saw . . . and inquired . . . and sent . . . and took." (11:2-4). At each point he might have conquered his lust. His look ought to have been checked (cf. Job 31:1, Matt. 5:27ff.). His enquiry revealed the fact that Bathsheba was married. The sin of adultery was forbidden by the seventh commandment (Exod. 20:14), and carried the death penalty (Lev. 20:10; Deut. 22:22). David saw, inquired, sent *and took*. This idea of sin's fatal progression is vividly illustrated in the Genesis narratives about Lot's sin at Sodom. First, he *looked* upon the city (Gen. 13:10). Then he *pitched his tent towards it* (Gen. 13:12f.). Within no time he was *inside it* (Gen. 14:12). Lot's sin began with an envious look. When the divine messengers came to deliver him from the evil city, no wonder they said: "*look not* behind thee" (Gen. 19:17). The angels knew how deadly a look could be (Gen. 19:26).

One of the pathetic things about this dreadful incident in David's life is his *futile attempt to cover his tracks* (11:6-13). By encouraging Uriah to go to his home David hoped that his own sin against his wife would not be revealed. The Bible clearly warns us of the stupidity of such hopes. All our sins are known to God. Everything is exposed to His gaze (Heb. 4:13; Ps. 139:1-7; Prov. 5:21). It is foolish to act as though He does not know about our sinning.

Notice also that the sinner will go *to almost any lengths to avoid exposure* (11:14ff.). The king reasoned that if Uriah was dead no questions would be asked about the birth of the child. David had already broken one commandment (Exod. 20:14); now he goes on to disobey another: "Thou shalt not kill" (Exod. 20:13). On that evening when the king gazed lustfully at Bathsheba he had no thought of murdering one of his most loyal army captains, but such is the way of sin.

## 2 BATHSHEBA—THE EQUALLY RESPONSIBLE PARTICIPANT

When we read this terrible story we instinctively think of the offence as David's sin, but this attractive woman cannot be entirely excused. Bathsheba was careless and foolish, lacking in the usual Hebrew modesty, or she certainly would not have washed in a place where she knew she could be overlooked. From her roof-top she would often have looked out to the royal palace and must have known that she could be seen. It is not enough merely to avoid sin *ourselves*. The New Testament insists that Christians must ensure that they do not become a stumbling block to others (Rom. 14:12-13). If David had gone to war he would not have seen Bathsheba that night. If she had thought seriously about her action she would not have put temptation in his path.

## 3 URIAH—THE INNOCENT SUFFERER

The action of the plot is made all the more offensive when we take note of the noble standards and high principles of David's captain, Uriah. When David's troops were summoned for battle Uriah had left his wife with no thought whatever of her possible unfaithfulness. As soon as David heard that Bathsheba was pregnant he sent for Uriah in the hope that the captain's stay in his own home would avert any suspicion of his wife's infidelity. But Uriah would not go into his house, probably because the soldiers had been "set apart" in a state of "holiness" for the prosecution of war. It was not fitting to break such a vow even though the king himself had suggested it.

Uriah had done nothing wrong but he was allowed to be

killed on the battlefield on the king's orders. An entirely innocent man was murdered in order to get David out of a serious moral difficulty.

## 4 JOAB—THE DANGEROUS ACCOMPLICE

Uriah's cruel death was made possible by Joab's co-operation. David ordered his commander to put Uriah in a dangerous place on the battlefield and then withdraw any support from him. Some time before, the king had lamented the fact that Joab had more power than was good for him or for the nation (2 Sam. 3:39). To give him more power by making such an evil request (11:14ff.) was an act of incredible folly. The army commander could always hold it against the king. But note that Joab did not carry out David's instructions to the letter. He knew that to have withdrawn support from Uriah would have a disastrous effect on the morale of the soldiers, so he initiated a move which he knew to be unwise and which would place scores of Uriah's fellow soldiers in equal danger. The sins of men inevitably affect the lives of many innocent people. A careful reading of the narrative reveals the fact that Bathsheba's husband was not the only innocent man to die as a result of David's transgression (11:17, 24).

## 5 NATHAN—THE VALIANT PROPHET

After reading so much about idleness, immorality, unfaithfulness and intrigue, it is like a breath of fresh air to find ourselves confronted by a fearless character such as Nathan. We read that Nathan obtained an audience with the king (2 Sam:12) and told him a simple parable about a wealthy yet greedy man who stole a small ewe lamb from a poor neighbour. One of the ideas behind the use of a parable was to trick the listener into an objective judgment or decision about the story before the self-appointed "judge" realized that he had passed sentence upon himself. David was quick to condemn. Hastily he took an oath and cried out in anger "As the Lord liveth, the man that hath done this thing shall surely die" (12:5). How accomplished we are at discerning and condemning the sins of others. With great skill and supreme artistry Nathan exposed the king's transgression. That blunt condemnation might easily have cost him his life. Over the past months there may well have been scandalous whispers at the royal court but nobody had had the courage to tell David about his sin. The child had already been born when Nathan went to David (12:14) and David had probably put these despicable acts of iniquity right out of his mind. For some time they may have troubled him but now his conscience had become utterly tranquil and undisturbed. We can live with our sins for such a long time that the shame of them hardly troubles us. Bishop Butler had a famous sermon on David's sin in this matter in which he spoke about David's "twelve months of self-deceit". From time to time most of us are guilty of insensitivity about our own sins. We make frequent efforts to overlook or ignore transgressions which we would not tolerate in others. In this connection, Psalm 19:12-13 ought to be used as a prayer. David realized that his "errors" were known to Nathan. Those "secret faults" had been exposed to all. His "presumptuous sins" were common knowledge throughout the court. He too was guilty of "the great transgression". His cry of penitence is found in an even more familiar psalm (Ps. 51) in which it becomes obvious that his longing for pardon is dominated by the thought that he has not only sinned against Bathsheba and Uriah, but against God Himself (Ps. 51:4).

It is easy for us to condemn David but can we be absolutely sure that, given those identical circumstances, we would not have committed that same sin? The story is not recorded to give us a sense of moral superiority. It should remind us of our absolute dependence upon God for power and create in us a sense of gratitude to Him for keeping us from such temptation. Augustine has a fine saying on this subject:

"O Pharisee, thou lovest little, because thou thinkest that

little has been forgiven thee ... 'What then,' quoth he, 'I who have never committed murder, am I to be deemed a murderer? I who have never committed adultery, am I to be punished for adultery?' ... But this saith unto thee thy God 'I was guiding thee for Myself, I was keeping thee for Myself. That thou shouldest not commit adultery, a tempter was absent: that a tempter should be absent, I brought it about. Place and time were lacking: and that these should be lacking, I brought it about. Suppose, on the contrary, that the tempter was there, and place and time were not wanting: that thou shouldest not consent, I terrified thee. Acknowledge therefore the grace of Him to whom thou owest that thou didst not commit this crime.' "

# 13

# MORE GRIEF AT HOME

Our next group of chapters (13:1–15:12) continues to illustrate the disastrous power of sin to reproduce itself in human life. When Nathan stood before the royal throne he boldly declared God's warning word of impending judgment (12:10-12), and this grim prophetic word was precisely fulfilled. Incest, hatred, murder, suspicion, jealousy and rebellion follow one after another. First we see David's immoral conduct with Bathsheba repeated in the behaviour of one of his sons (13:1-22) whilst the remaining verses of the chapter (the murder of Amnon, 13:23-39) recall David's cruel treatment of Uriah. The serious words of the apostle Paul are surely relevant here: "Whatsoever a man soweth, that shall he also reap" (Gal. 6:7).

The central character in these chapters is David's son, Absalom, and we take note of five things about him:

## 1 ABSALOM'S BACKGROUND

We are told that he was the son of the princess Maacah, the daughter of Talmai, King of Geshur (2 Sam. 3:3). Geshur was an Aramaean state, north-easet of the Sea of Galilee, but God's Word expressly forbade marriage with non-Israelites. If David had been obedient to the revealed will of God he would not have married such an unbelieving person (Joshua 23:12-13 cf. Deut. 7:3). Such marriages were often measures of political convenience and were used to strengthen foreign alliances, but even if David felt that it was quite in order to marry the foreign princess, the laws of kingship (Deut. 17:14-17) forbade the multiplication of wives. It does seem that at these points David was deliberately disobedient to the Law of God and the final result was increasing sorrow. But for David's disobedience in the matter of mixed marriages the tragedy of Absalom's rebellion might never have happened. There is scarcely anything in the Christian life more important than obedience (cf. John 2:5; 15:14). With such a sad background of disobedience and ungodly association Absalom's evil character is hardly surprising.

## 2 ABSALOM'S BITTERNESS

Absalom was determined to kill Amnon because of the way he had treated his sister, but for two full years he waited his opportunity, and continued to harbour this bitter hatred in his heart. He knew that at some time in the future he would discover the best moment to get his revenge (13:22-23). If David had been in a position to punish Amnon for his sin against the girl, Tamar, this bitterness might not have built itself up in Absalom's heart and mind. But how could David discipline Amnon; his own sin condemned him and produced bitter fruit in the lives of his children. Both Amnon's sensuality and Absalom's ruthless killing were sins that the sons had learned from their father. Of course, Absalom was not free from blame. It was bad enough that Amnon had sinned. To maintain an unforgiving, revengeful spirit would inevitably lead to further sorrow and anguish. If we become resentful or bitter towards anyone, we rob ourselves of the priceless blessing of communion with God (cf. Ps. 66:18).

As a result of his action, Absalom fled from the country (13:37-38), but his father became terribly grieved during his absence from court and his military captain, Joab, arranged a plot to make Absalom's return possible. The story of the woman of Tekoah (14:1-20) is of great interest. Once again David finds himself "trapped by a tale". As in the Nathan parable he pronounces judgment before he realizes that he is passing sentence upon himself. Absalom is allowed to return to Jerusalem but David soon recognizes that the cunning mind of Joab is behind the events (14:19-21).

### 3 ABSALOM'S PRIDE

The prince returned to Israel but was not encouraged to enter the royal palace and for two years he stayed in his own house. We know little about his activities at this time but the biblical narrative does provide us with an important detail about his personal life. A man of outstanding physical beauty, he also appears to have been incredibly arrogant and obsessed with self-admiration (14:25-26). Obviously proud of his hair, it ultimately became the cause of his death (18:9). Scripture has a good deal to say about the awful danger of pride in our lives. The Book of Proverbs is particularly concerned about its perils (e.g. 11:2; 13:10; 16:18; 29:23).

### 4 ABSALOM'S INGRATITUDE

Absalom was grieved because he had not been given an audience at the royal court (14:28) and begged Joab to put in a good word for him so that he might return to an influential position in the royal household. Because Joab refused to cooperate, Absalom set fire to Joab's fields in order to make him do something for him. What an ungrateful and desperately selfish type of man Absalom was.

### 5 ABSALOM'S INTRIGUE

Ultimately Absalom was given a royal audience and as soon as David saw him he was quickly reinstated in the royal favour. Once assured of a secure position at court, Absalom planned to usurp his father's authority and take the crown for himself. He did this by a series of cunning acts. First he provided himself with a well-equipped personal bodyguard (15:1). This was often the first step of a man who planned to get to the throne (cf. 1 Kgs. 1:5). Then Absalom feigned an intense interest in the private affairs of the people (15:2-4). The final stage in his plot was to suggest to his father that he be permitted to honour a spiritual vow he was supposed to have made whilst in Geshur. He obtained his wishes by covering his evil ambitions with a cloak of religious intention (15:7). He was given permission to go to Hebron and he went on his way surrounded by a couple of hundred eager admirers who had no idea that they were playing a vital part in a national revolution. They "went in their simplicity and they knew not anything" (15:11). There are always simple people who will blindly follow the latest fashion or idea without stopping to think out the serious implications of their actions. These folk did not realize that in following Absalom they were turning their back on a king who loved them. The trumpets sounded in various parts of the country and hundreds of foolish people cried out exultantly "Absalom reigneth in Hebron". They had been subtly manipulated by an unscrupulous leader and, had they but known it, were initiating the saddest event in David's life.

# 14

# FRIENDS IN NEED

The passages to which we now turn (15:13–17:29) contain some of the most exciting material in the life of David. In his time David had obviously been a strong personality and yet, at the moment when he was in such need, it was quite ordinary people in the community who came to help him. This particular section of the narrative gives us some vivid word-pictures of a number of people who stood by the exiled king during Absalom's rebellion; it reveals some fascinating character studies, and suggests some qualities expected of Christians in our own day. We too have mutual responsibility for the spiritual welfare of one another (Gal. 6:2; Rom. 15:1). When we study David's friends at this critical time in his life and admire their lovely qualities, one of the serious disadvantages is that we know the *end* of the story. We know that ultimately David was the victor and got back to Jerusalem, but when the king's friends left the city with him they did not know that. It might well have turned out differently and instead of Absalom hanging in a tree, they might have been the people who were hung. This is one of the things we are apt to forget, because we know the full story. They had no idea how the episode would end and their loyalty might easily have cost them their lives.

There are five people, or groups of people, who demand our attention:

I THE SERVANTS WHO TRUSTED THE KING'S WISDOM (2 Sam. 15:13-17)
The king realized that Absalom was bound to march on Jerusalem. David had fortified the city and made it a strong and

impressive capital. He cherished an intense love for Jerusalem and its people, and could not bear the thought that this beautiful place might be destroyed in any kind of conflict, civil war or revolution. The servants replied to the king's orders with words which ought often to be on our own lips: "thy servants are ready to do whatsoever my lord the king shall appoint" (15:15). They were ordinary members of the royal household and, of course, had no rights of their own (cf. 1 Cor. 6:19). Their duty at that moment was to obey the king's instructions and to trust his wisdom. It meant that they were going into a life of hardship, insecurity, privation, suffering and possibly death, but *they would be with the king*, and that was enough. The striking parallels to our own voluntary surrender to the Lord Jesus are obvious. There are several New Testament references which provide us with striking evidence of this same kind of spirit within the early church. There is the same grateful surrender which we have seen in David's servants and there is something exhilarating and exciting about the fearless dedication of the early Christians and their gay abandonment to God's sovereign purpose for their lives (cf. Acts 5:41; 1 Peter 4:13ff.; 2 Cor. 4:11, 17). God sometimes calls us to difficult assignments, but His will is best, and one day we shall understand the reason for our hardships. David's servants trusted the word of the king, and though they were not able to sort out all the intricacies of the revolution and what exactly was going on in national affairs, they just came in a spirit of resignation and glad obedience: "We are ready to do whatsoever my lord the king shall appoint."

We frequently need to remind ourselves that the New Testament epistles were also written in times of crisis to people whose homes had been plundered, who had lost their precious belongings, but who rejoiced in it all because they were assured that in heaven they had a better and an enduring substance (Heb. 10:34). In some parts of the world today our fellow Christians pay a high price for their faith. Is the quality of our faith rich enough for this? Or do we only talk about being prepared to do whatsoever the king shall appoint whilst in fact that faith and commitment of ours has never been tested in crisis, and if it were it might be found weak and insecure?

## 2 THE SOLDIER WHO WANTED THE KING'S COMPANIONSHIP (2 Sam. 18-22)

We now look at Ittai, the Gittite. This man was a Gentile as were so many of David's helpers, so he did not have a *religious* allegiance which bound him to either king or nation. Like the other servants, Ittai came to David in his trouble because he was so deeply attracted to David *as a man*. The passage records the words of David to this loyal soldier: "Wherefore goest thou also with us? return to thy place, and abide with the king: for thou art a stranger, and also an exile. Whereas thou camest but yesterday, should I this day make thee go up and down with us? seeing I go whither I may, return thou, and take back thy brethren: mercy and truth be with thee." Ittai answered David in memorable words: "Surely in what place my lord the king shall be, whether in death or life, even there also will thy servant be."

It is interesting to note that here was a Philistine, a man from Gath, who had an intense love for David and was prepared to sacrifice comfort and security in order to be in his company. He could have been assured of a good place in Absalom's new army because he was an accomplished soldier but he was not prepared to leave David. We must remind ourselves that Ittai spoke these words at a time when David's fortunes were at their lowest. It was an act of voluntary consecration, made in the presence of others. Such loyalty to a human king ought to encourage our utter devotion to the King of Kings. Some great exhortations or commands in the Epistle to the Romans, chapters 6 and 12, remind us that the same kind of thing is expected from us as Christians—yield yourselves (6:13), present your bodies

(12:1). These are the believer's orders from the Eternal King.

### 3 THE PRIESTS WHO OBEYED THE KING'S INSTRUCTIONS (2 Sam. 15:23-30)

Let us look now at the priests who walked alongside David on the day he left Jerusalem. Many of the people who witnessed this march of the exiles "wept with a loud voice". David was a fugitive, leading his servants out into the wilderness. Zadok the priest, and all the Levities, "set down the ark of God" and, at that moment, David urged the priests to carry the ark of God back to Jerusalem. David had the assurance that if he found favour in the eyes of the Lord, He would bring him home again. Then, in words of memorable resignation, he said: "But if he thus say, I have no delight in thee; behold here am I, let him do to me as seemeth good unto him." Zadok and Abiathar obeyed David's instructions and took the ark back into the city and the exiled king continued his journey, weeping as he went out into a desperately uncertain future. David's words to the priests express something of his own acute sense of reliance upon God and his willingness to accept the will of God for his life whatever it might be.

These verses illustrate David's concern for the spiritual life of his people. He wanted the ark to be in Jerusalem and not with him. It was an outward symbol to the people of God's abiding presence. They could not possibly be indifferent about its location. Its presence was regarded as a sign of God's approval so, as the priests carried the ark, they were saying in effect, "if we have the ark with us we are safe and secure." But the dominant thing in David's mind was the spiritual welfare of his people. It was not only that he, personally, was willing to resign himself completely to God; he had a deep concern about spiritual issues. He knew, in fact, that the "take over" in the city was not going to be on the side of true "religion". The things of God did not count for much with Absalom. David knew, for example, that the new king who was about to establish himself had precious little religious commitment or faith in God, and would not be likely to lead the people in the ways of godliness. So David thought, "At least then let us leave the priests. Let us hope that in some way, even though I am going to lose my place in the kingdom, the work of communicating the truth of God will still go on." When we try to enter into the Hebrew mind and realize how important the ark was to them, we realize that for David to say, "You take the ark back to the city," was one of the greatest moments in his religious life. In other words, he was saying: "my dominant concern is not my *personal* welfare. What matters most is that the truth of God shall go on, and I can trust God whether I have the symbolism or not." That was an immense step forward for a man at that particular stage in religious development. The other thing, of course, is that Zadok and his fellow priests were not lacking in courage either. They would feel far more secure in exile with a devout man like David than with a godless man in the city. They knew from their own history what happened to priests when godless kings came to power. Few of them could forget about Saul and the priests at Nob. It was an extremely courageous action to go back to the city, but they went simply because they wanted to do the will of a man they recognized as the true king.

It is not always easy to say "yes" to the will of our Great King, but it is best. Obedience is often costly and it demands courage but it brings its own rich reward and, like the priests, our dominant concern must always be the continuation of the work of God and the communication of the word of God to other people, not our own personal welfare. So often, instead of helping forward that work by our sacrificial service and by yielding ourselves, we hinder it because we are too concerned about our own ideas, our own comfort and self-preservation.

## 4 THE FRIENDS WHO ENTERED THE KING'S SERVICE (2 Sam. 15:32-37)

In these verses we note that a group of valiant people were willing to share in the exceptionally dangerous mission of getting information about Absalom's plans back to David's encampment. An old man named Hushai agreed to be the spy. Because of his age and experience he would probably be admitted to Absalom's "Council of War". The plan was that Hushai would tell the priests, Zadok and Abiathar, and they in turn would ask their sons to get the news to David's camp. Delivering such a message was an errand which required immense courage for they were sure to be watched. We read the outworking of this story in Chapter 17:5-22, and notice that they *were* seen; a thrilling adventure followed.

It was not just one person who shared in this enterprise. A group of people united to play a part together. There was Hushai, Zadok and Abiathar, an unknown girl who took the message, Jonathan and Ahimaaz, who actually ran the errand, and an unnamed woman who had the courage to hide the two messengers in a disused well. There are many different people who play their part in service for the Lord. In any successful Christian venture the number of active workers is immense and no man can take all the credit to himself. Behind every personal confession of faith in the Lord Jesus as Saviour, there is somebody praying, somebody giving some literature, somebody taking an interest, somebody just being kind for Christ's sake, somebody issuing an invitation to a service, somebody making them feel at home in church. Surely, this is one of the things the Lord Jesus has in mind when He says "other men laboured, and ye are entered into their labours" (John 4:37-38). Paul says that one man plants and another man waters (1 Cor. 3: 6-10). There are all types of people with a variety of different gifts who play a part in our spiritual life, and all are important. Every one of these friends who served King David in this way had this in common, their different tasks required immense courage; their service might easily have cost them their lives.

## 5 THE MEN WHO SUPPLIED THE KING'S NEEDS (2 Sam. 17:27-29)

The exiled king took his tired men across the river Jordan. It was an escape route and very soon they would be pursued. "And it came to pass when David was come to Mahanaim, that Shobi, the son of Nahash of Rabbah of the children of Ammon, and Machir the son of Ammiel of Lo-debar, and Barzillai the Gileadite of Rogelim brought beds, and basons, and earthen vessels, and wheat, and barley, and flour and parched corn and beans, and lentils, and parched pulse, and honey, and butter, and sheep, and cheese of kine, for David, and for the people that were with him to eat: for they said, The people is hungry, and weary, and thirsty, in the wilderness" (17:27-29). These three men came out to meet the king with their provisions. The place of meeting was familiar to every Hebrew. Its name was Mahanaim, the place where the angels met Jacob—the "angels" were coming again but this time in the person of the three men! Each of them might have stayed at home and offered excuses instead of presenting gifts. Moreover, if Absalom came to power they could pay for this loyalty with their lives. We shall think about the excuses they might well have made rather than go out to meet the fugitive.

The first man was *Shobi*, "the son of Nahash of Rabbah of the children of Ammon". It was against the Ammonites that David had organized a successful military campaign (2 Sam. 11:1). We recall that a serious tribal feud had started because of the way the new king of Ammon (Shobi's brother) had disgraced David's messengers and sent them back with torn clothes and shorn beards. Shobi might well have said: "This man does not deserve kindness; the last act he did towards my people was a cruel one. I am glad this has happened to him." But he refused to think like that. He may even have been ashamed of his brother's treatment of David's ambassadors. David's plight presented him with a glorious opportunity to demonstrate his own desire for peace and friendship. Perhaps we do not take nearly seriously enough our opportunities for generosity and kindness as a way of overcoming difficulties in relationships. This is surely what the apostle Paul meant when he said "If thine enemy hunger feed him" (Rom. 12:20). The New Testament insists that no matter how much anybody persecutes us we are to go out of our way to serve that one in practical Christian love.

*Machir*, the second friend, could have offered an excellent excuse. He might have said, "I have done my share of good works." He was the man who had given a home to Mephibosheth for many years (9:4). Now, confronted with these tired exiles, he might easily have said "I have done my bit." But he did not react to David's plight in that way. He eagerly grasped a fresh opportunity for service. We must not use our past achievements or former work for God as an excuse for getting out of our present responsibilities. We still have further opportunities for service to other people in the name of Christ.

The third friend, *Barzillai*, might well have said, "I am far too old to be of help," for he was over eighty years old. He could have protested, "I would love to help but I do not have the energy and spirit to do it." But he loved the king so much that he refused to offer that kind of weak excuse. He put himself out and made the sacrifice. Barzillai is an encouragement to all elderly people. He tells us that, whatever our age, there are things we can still do to show our love for the King.

These wonderful people form part of a long line of valiant pilgrims who have served God and His people in one way or another over the centuries. Their courageous and sacrificial service ought to inspire and challenge us all to greater devotion and more heroic ventures for Him.

# 15

# THE KING COMES HOME

The next group of chapters provide an account of Absalom's defeat and death and tell of King David's return to power (2 Sam. 18-21). We shall consider their message under four headings:

## 1 THE KING'S PROBLEM

We quickly discover that, although Absalom's army was defeated, the military victory owed little to David; it was due solely to his ruthless army commander, Joab. It soon became obvious that King David was no longer the power in the land. The control of national affairs was really in the treacherous and unscrupulous hands of Joab. The biblical narratives make it clear that the king had many military captains who were a great strength and encouragement to him (1 Chr. 11:15ff., for example), but Joab could hardly be included among them. He was self-centred, ambitious and corrupt. The king had made a great mistake in giving him too much control, but as Joab was his nephew it was difficult to do much about it. In his study of Bible characters, Alexander Whyte has some incisive things to say about Joab. He observes that ". . . had it not been for David, Joab would have climbed up into the throne of Israel. As it was, he stood on the steps of the throne and faced the King all his days . . . even the King himself was afraid of his commander-in-chief . . . Joab was King in all but the crown, King and more. But as long as his weaker uncle wore the crown, Joab's heart raged like hell . . ." Dr. Whyte also draws a contrast between Joab and Jonathan: "Jonathan gave over to David all that he possessed, and died a King. Joab envied

David and everyone else all that they had, and died an out-cast ..." We are told a number of sinister things about David's cruel nephew. The narrative reveals:

### (a) Joab's heartless disobedience (18:5, 11, 14)

David had given clear instructions regarding the way Absalom was to be treated, but Joab deliberately disobeyed the king and mercilessly slew his son. The king would have had to punish Absalom, of course, and would probably have sent his son into exile again, but Joab would not give David the opportunity to display such mercy.

### (b) Joab's awful reputation (18:11-13)

The soldier who reported that Absalom was hanging, caught by his long hair in an oak tree, knew exactly how unscrupulous Joab was. When Joab said that if he had killed Absalom he would have given him ten shekels of silver and a valuable girdle, the soldier replied "thou thyself wouldest have set thyself against me". How dreadful to be so obviously vindictive and unloving that people can easily plot your next cruel move!

### (c) Joab's unhelpful power (19:1-8)

Joab slew Absalom but, when he returned to the city as a victor, he was annoyed to find that, such was the people's love for David, the whole community shared the king's anguish about Absalom's death. But Joab was the real king now and issued his orders to David: "Now therefore arise, go forth . . . for I swear by the Lord, if thou go not forth, there will not tarry one with thee this night: and that will be worse unto thee than all the evil that befell thee from thy youth until now." David was powerless at that moment. Joab was the cruel master of the situation. Many good people are ruined by the unhelpful influence of those who are "behind them". David would have been a far better man without the help of his nephew.

*(d) Joab's appalling treachery* (19:9-14; 20:1-26)

By this time David knew that Joab was no good to him but he was far too late in making the discovery. As an attempt to free himself from his nephew's tyranny he aimed to replace him by Amasa, the man who had led Absalom's armies (19:13; cf. 17:25). Sheba, a soldier from the tribe of Benjamin (and therefore a member of the pro-Saul party) led a strong opposition group against David, and the king sent Amasa, instead of Joab, to quell the rising (20:1-7). Joab soon grasped the significance of what was happening and almost exactly repeated the incident of Abner's slaughter (20:8-10). Joab cut down anybody who was in his way. Abner, Absalom, Amasa were all a threat to him and he did not rest until they were removed.

2 THE KING'S RETURN

The exiled king made his way back to his own capital and it is interesting to note the men who were present to welcome him back. Three individuals are mentioned by name at this point in the story:

*Shimei* was at the river bank with his pathetic cry for forgiveness (19:16-23). He was a member of Saul's family circle and on the day the king left Jerusalem Shimei had cursed David and hurled stones at him (16:5f.). Now he came begging for mercy and pardon. Shimei is typical of the man who is hasty and careless in his conversation. He now regretted all he had said and admitted that he had sinned (19:20), but his cry of penitence did not take the sting out of his former cruel words. Proverbs has much to teach us about unkind and hasty speech and its perilous consequences (4:24; 6:12-14; 10:32).

*Mephibosheth* was not much better. It is sad to see how insensitive he was to David's needs when Absalom's army was marching against Jerusalem. Years before, the king had welcomed him into the royal palace and fully provided for him (9:1-13) but when David was in trouble he would not stand by him (16:3). Mephibosheth vigorously protested his loyalty and insisted that his servant, Ziba, had slandered and misrepresented him to the king (19:24-30). In reading the narrative, it is not possible to be dogmatic about who was telling the truth, but David certainly showed a forgiving spirit to both of them.

Barzillai was the most attractive of the three (19:31-39). Over eighty years of age, he came to pay his respects to the returning king. He had no ulterior motive in meeting David by the riverside. As a mark of his keen gratitude for the help Barzillai had given to him, David offered him a place of special privilege and honour in the Jerusalem palace. But the old man refused the gift; it was enough that his king had returned safely.

These three very different men are a study in themselves. Shimei had been an obvious opponent of the king. Barzillai had been an eager helper. Of Mephibosheth's true loyalty we cannot be sure, but doubtless the king knew the truth. We Christian people have an "exiled King". The unbelieving world cried: "Away with Him . . . crucify Him" (John 19:15). Throughout the centuries there have been those who have cried: "We will not have this man to reign over us" (Luke 19:14). But our King is coming back. How will we meet Him at His glorious return? (Matt. 25:31ff.; 16:27). With remorse like Shimei, excuses like Mephibosheth, or with a deep sense of profound joy and gratitude like the aged Barzillai?

### 3 THE KING'S LIMITATIONS

The story which follows (2 Samuel 21) raises some problems. It reminds us that these devout Old Testament personalities can never be our highest examples, for they were often guilty of terribly cruel acts. This leads us to a most important aspect of biblical interpretation: these people walked in all the light they knew and were quite obviously conditioned by the thought-forms of their own day. Every book of the Bible needs the other books as its interpreters. It is important to understand that such an act of blood-revenge as that recorded in 2 Samuel 21:1-14 would be quite consistent with the political and religious behaviour of David's contemporaries. There is development, however, in the Old Testament itself as God's servants received fresh insight into God's mind and will. At this time the People of God were in their religious infancy. You cannot teach everything to a child in one day; it takes time for light and insight to come to the understanding mind. David's retributive slaughter of the grandchildren of Saul makes sad reading for us, but this was how they viewed life in those times. Its merit was that it took sin *seriously*. It recognized that no man (or tribe) could hope to sin and escape punishment. The Old Testament is a preparatory revelation and keenly looks forward to a time when God will reveal Himself and His purposes in fuller measure. That eagerly awaited revelation came in Christ. He looked back on these stories and thought about David's leadership of the nation with a deep sense of gratitude, but He gave us a far better word about the treatment of our enemies (Matt. 5:38-48; Luke 6:27-36; cf. Rom. 12:14; 1 Peter 2:23; 3:9).

## 4 THE KING'S WEAKNESS

By now David was obviously feeling his age and we see something of the deep respect and devotion accorded him throughout the nation (21:15ff.). The people regarded him as "the light of Israel". In its time the lamp of his life had shone with clear brightness into many a dark situation, but now the light was flickering. The king's long and fruitful life was nearing its end.

# 16

# THE END OF A GREAT ERA

The closing scenes of David's life are now portrayed (2 Samuel 22 to 1 Kings 2:10). The reign had been an outstanding one. David had made mistakes and, like most of us, would have coveted the opportunity of re-living some of the scenes. However, despite his errors, the king had ruled well, but his throne was far from secure. The close of this great era is characterized by disobedience, rebellion, intrigue and bitterness, and it is almost as though the historian, himself, is reminding us of the transient nature of all earthly things. The narrative illustrates again man's tragic tendency to prefer evil to good and his almost incurable self-centredness and pride. We take note of five themes:

## I PERSONAL THANKSGIVING
As the Second Book of Samuel reaches its climax it draws us away from rivalry and ambition and shows us the spiritually exultant king pouring out his heart in deep gratitude to the God who has safely led him all his days. In this psalm, David expresses his profound thanksgiving to the Ever-Faithful God for:

### (a) Security (22:2-20)
It is fascinating to see how things from everyday life reminded David of God's faithfulness. As a fugitive he had often sheltered in the rocky caves in the wilderness and, similarly, God had been his refuge ("my Rock", 22:2-3, cf. Psa. 61:2-3). On dangerous military encounters he had relied on his strong shield and this spoke to him of a better Pro-rector. Huge fortresses and high towers were places of sanc-

tuary and so he rejoiced that in dark days God had fortified his soul (22:2-3). He had been through terrifying experiences but out of the depths of his heart could cry: "the Lord was my stay" (22:19). Fearful of some dangerous situations he had proved that even there the Lord had "prevented" or gone before him (22:19).

### (b) Mercy (22:21-29)
The king knew how deeply in the past he had cast himself on the loving kindness and mercy of God. He likens God Himself to a lamp or candle in a dark place, an echo of Psalm 119 where God's Word is likened to a lamp. Doubtless David recalled those times when God had entered into his darkest moments with the brightness of His own unchanging Presence. He remembered with gratitude the light of His pardoning mercy after his cruel sin against Bathsheba and Uriah, and knew that a God who met such need would not fail him in the future.

### (c) Power (22:30-51)
Once a man is forgiven he needs supernatural power to prevent his falling again in the same way. The next section of the psalm rejoices in the God who makes a man adequate for every situation and girds him with strength (22:40).

### (d) Guidance (23:1-7)
David knew that the responsibilities of national leadership were too great for him but he rejoiced in the assurance that God had given him clear directions about how to rule his people "in the fear of God" (23:3).

### 2 FAMILY GRIEF
As a king David was wonderfully helped but he had encountered serious troubles in his own home. 23:5 is a difficult verse to translate but if we follow the renderings in the Authorized and Revised Versions it is possible to discern

here a hint about David's sadness regarding the ungodly members of his family: "Although my house be not so with God" (AV) or "Verily my house is not so with God" (RV). Possibly the king recognized that he was not entirely free from blame in this matter. At times he might have been a better example. *Absalom* led a revolution against his father and was a tragic disappointment. *Adonijah's* life was characterized by passionate self-seeking (1 Kgs. 1:5); he struggled to get on the throne before his father had died. *Solomon* began well but was equally selfish and brought immense grief to the nation and to God (1 Kgs. 11:6-9; 12:4). Every believing man and woman has to battle against difficulties in at least one area of their lives. David's heaviest burden was not in shouldering national affairs but in bearing domestic grief.

## 3 NATIONAL PRIDE

Chapter 24 of 2 Samuel relates David's sin of numbering the people. His demand for a census is generally regarded as a sad indication of his *pride*. It is one of the very rare occasions when Joab tried to be an influence for good (24:3) but the king's arrogant ambition had to be satisfied and even Joab's pleading was in vain.

## 4 COURT INTRIGUE

The old king's reign drew to a close with a tragic sequence of events. Adonijah, with Joab as his supporter, attempted to take the crown (1 Kings 1:5-9). The popular acclamation received by David's nominated successor, Solomon, was largely due to the people's devotion to David and their great respect for Nathan the prophet. Both sons had leading priests on their side, but religious support for a cause means nothing. Religious leaders can be just as mistaken as anybody else.

Our last word arises out of one intensely disappointing aspect of David's last days—his order regarding Shimei. It serves as a reminder that David himself needed greater light. His outstanding life can teach us many lessons, but we must always remember that God's finest word to us is not from the life of any mere man. However noble and virtuous he may be, he will still be a man, with a man's failings, mistakes, perverse judgments and selfish ambitions. The Shimei incident showed how merciful David could be (2 Sam. 18:18-23) but his dying wish (1 Kgs. 2:8ff.) was for vengeance on the man he had forgiven, and all this is a far cry from the teaching of the Lord Jesus (Matt. 5:44; cf. Rom. 12:19ff.). The Old Testament has much to say to us, and lessons of permanent value will emerge from a serious study of its contents, but we shall always be left crying out for the One it anticipates.

The opening words of the Epistle to the Hebrews express the truth magnificently when they say that "God who at sundry times and in divers manners spake in time past unto the fathers by the prophets, hath in these last days spoken unto us by his Son." These great Old Testament characters walked in all the light they knew but their insight was partial, fragmentary and restricted. We ought ever to be thankful for the fulness of revelation which is ours in Christ. In any serious study of the Old Testament all roads lead ultimately to the Lord Jesus. If the Holy Spirit is our Teacher, a survey of David's life ought to drive us to David's Lord.

Within the Book of Psalms there is a group of magnificent hymns (73-83) written by Asaph. One of these (78) relates the story of God's gracious dealings with His people in history and it closes with a superb reference to David. It tells how he was chosen by God for national leadership, and skilfully compares his ministry as a shepherd with his service as king. God took the skilful hands of an ordinary shepherd and used them that His people might be graciously fed and safely directed. David's example remains a rich encouragement to us all, but we are in the stronger Hands of an even better Shepherd. He will feed us and firmly lead us until, like David, we too are "in the house of the Lord for ever".